D1760652

SHADOW WARRIORS

THE IRISH ARMY RANGER WING

PAUL O'BRIEN &
WAYNE FITZGERALD

MERCIER PRESS

It is Army Ranger Wing policy to neither confirm nor deny the information contained within this book. Furthermore, for reasons of national security, and for the protection of ongoing operations and protection of persons, it is Army Ranger Wing policy not to discuss past or present operations.

MERCIER PRESS

Cork

www.mercierpress.ie

© Paul O'Brien and Wayne Fitzgerald, 2020

ISBN: 978 1 78117 762 4

A CIP record for this title is available from the British Library.

Printed and bound in the EU.

The ARW motto:

Glaine ár gCroí, Neart ár nGéag,
Agus beart de réir ár mbriathar.

(The cleanliness of our hearts, the strength of our limbs,
and our commitment to our promise.)

Dedicated to those who have served in the
Army Ranger Wing, who are currently serving,
and who will serve in the future.

CONTENTS

ABBREVIATIONS 7

INTRODUCTION 11

GENESIS

  1. WARS WITHOUT FRONTS 16

  2. INCEPTION 23

  3. 'WE ARE RANGERS' 30

  4. THE SPECIAL ASSAULT GROUP 38

  5. THE ARMY RANGER WING 44

  6. TRIAL AND ERROR 52

  7. AID TO THE CIVIL POWER 60

  8. THE LONG WAR 65

LAND, SEA AND EVERYWHERE

  9. THE ARW OVERSEAS 72

  10. SOMALIA 80

  11. EAST TIMOR 87

  12. LIBERIA 94

  13. CHAD 101

  14. MALI 107

WHAT WE DO IN THE SHADOWS

  15. MAKING THE CUT TODAY 114

16. In the Cross Hairs 122

17. By Neptune's Beard 129

18. Drop Zone 134

19. Close Quarter Battle 139

20. Bí Úllamh 144

Conclusion 149

Appendix: 'So you want to pass selection ...' 151

Bibliography 155

Recommended Reading 156

Acknowledgements 158

ABBREVIATIONS

AHQ	Army Headquarters
AML	Panard-type vehicle
AO	Area of Operations
APC	Armoured Personnel Carrier
ARW	Army Ranger Wing
C2 group	Command & Control
CAR	Central African Republic
CEMO	Combat Equipment Marching Order
Comms	Communications
CP	Close Protection
CPT	Close Protection Team
CQB	Close Quarter Battle
CRRC	Combat Rubber Raiding Craft
CSDP	Common Security and Defence Policy
CT	Counter-terrorism
CTR	Close Target Recce
DF	Defence Forces
DS	Directing Staff
ECOWAS	Economic Community of West African States
EOD	Explosive Ordnance Disposal

ERV	Escape Rendezvous
EU	European Union
FN	Fabrique Nationale
FOB	Forward Operating Base
FRV	Forward Rendezvous
G8	Group of Eight (an inter-governmental political forum, now G7)
GIGN	Groupe d'intervention de la Gendarmerie nationale (elite tactical unit of the French National Police)
GOL	Government of Liberia
GPMG	General Purpose Machine Gun
GSG 9	Grenzschutzgruppe 9
HALO	High Altitude Low Opening
HMG	Heavy Machine Gun
HQ	Headquarters
IEDs	Improvised Explosive Devices
INLA	Irish National Liberation Army
INTERFET	International Force East Timor
IR	Infra-red strobe lights
IRA	Irish Republican Army
IWW	Infantry Weapons Wing
LFTT	Live Fire Tactical Training
Lt	Lieutenant
LURD	Liberians United for Reconciliation and Democracy

MINURCAT	United Nations Mission in the Central African Republic and Chad
MINUSMA	United Nations Multidimensional Integrated Stabilization Mission in Mali
MO	Medical Officer
MODEL	Movement for Democracy in Liberia
MOLLE	Modular Lightweight Load-Carrying Equipment
MOUT	Military Operations in Urban Terrain
NCO	Non-commissioned Officer
NSV	Russian-manufactured machine gun
NVE	Night Vision Equipment
NVG	Night Vision Goggles
O/C	Officer Commanding
OP	Observation Post
PCM	An Para-Chumann Mileata
PDF	Permanent Defence Forces
PT	Physical Training
PTI	Physical Training Instructor
QRF	Quick Reaction Force
Recce	Reconnaissance
Retd	Retired
RIB	Rigid Inflatable Boat
RPG	Rocket-propelled Grenade
RSM	Regimental Sergeant Major
RTA	Reaction to Attack

RTU	Returned To Unit
SAG	Special Assault Group
SAS	Special Air Service
Sec	Section
SERE	Survival Evasion Resistance Extraction
SFP	Sustainable Function Programme
SIGINT	Signals Intelligence
SO	Senior Officer
SOF	Special Operations Force
SOFQ	Special Operations Force Qualification
SOPs	Standard Operating Procedures
SOTG	Special Operations Task Group
SRV	Special Reconnaissance Vehicles
TACCOM	Tactical Communications
TL	Team Leader
TTPs	Tactics, Techniques and Procedures
UN	United Nations
UNAMET	United Nations Mission in East Timor
UNIFIL	United Nations Interim Force in Lebanon
UNITAF	Unified Task Force
UNMIL	United Nations Mission in Liberia
UNOSOM	United Nations Operation in Somalia

INTRODUCTION

Special forces have played an important role throughout history, with specialist units operating covertly and overtly in a number of conflicts. The origin of such forces can be traced back as far as the likes of the Roman Praetorian Guard and the Anglo-Saxon Huscarls at the Battle of Hastings, and can also be seen in Cromwell's Ironsides, Napoleon's Old Guard, and the French Foreign Legion. As the centuries progressed and warfare developed, many of these groups were amalgamated into their country's regular forces, but in times of war there is always a need for improvisation, meaning that today's special forces will often work outside the purview of the regular forces.

Contrary to popular belief, a special forces operative is not the gung-ho, weapon-toting figure often portrayed on the silver screen, but a highly trained and very skilled soldier. Modern elite soldiers have a wide array of skills, both physical and intellectual. They have been trained in this manner due to the emergence of a new type of warfare in the mid-to-late twentieth century: the increase in national and international terrorism.

The Irish Army Ranger Wing (ARW) was formed by

the Irish government and the Department of Defence during the spring of 1980 and is affectionately known as 'The Wing'. Those who set out the initial ARW course back in 1980 had by then witnessed over a decade of this new type of warfare. In fact, it was in response to the ever-increasing terrorist attacks throughout the world in the late 1960s and early 1970s that many countries created their specialist units. The hijacking of planes, high-profile assassinations and the 1972 Munich massacre in Germany brought home the fact that, with terrorism, there were no defined battle fronts and civilians were often caught up in the fray. However, it was events in the North of Ireland in the late 1960s and 1970s in particular that found the Irish Defence Forces needing to adapt to a new and demanding period within its history.

Special forces, such as the ARW, exist to conduct special operations, irregular warfare, and counter-insurgency and counter-terrorism (CT) operations. The instructors who trained that first cadre of ARW operatives in 1980 had themselves, since the late 1960s, undergone a number of specialist courses, both at home and abroad, to ensure they could ably train and cultivate elite soldiers. This training, as well as their belief in the potential of the ARW, ensured that those in The Wing would be able to tackle some of the most difficult physical and mental challenges that a soldier could encounter while on specialist operations. As with similar special operations forces (SOFs) throughout the world, the ARW has undergone training to conduct counter-hijack operations, hostage rescue, airborne and seaborne interventions, search missions, pursuit, recapture of terrorist-held objectives, close protection, and contingency planning to counteract planned terrorist or subversive threats.

The first overseas course that members of the ARW attended was an anti-terrorism intervention course run by Groupe d'intervention de la Gendarmerie nationale (GIGN) in Paris in 1981. Since then, the ARW has fostered a number of relationships with SOF and specialist counter-terrorism police units around the world, conducting regular exchanges and training courses. This enables it to continue to operate at a high level of proficiency at home and abroad in the protection of the state and its people.

In writing the story of the ARW, we have respected the wishes of those serving and those who have served by not including details of covert operations, names of those involved on those missions, or any other sensitive intelligence. As the reader will appreciate, there is much which cannot and should not be published in terms of names, tactics and procedures lest it provide an advantage for a future terrorist. Moreover, many of the operations that involved the ARW are covered by the Official Secrets

Act and it would, therefore, be illegal to disclose these to the public. Although, in recent years, many stories have circulated via social media about The Wing, on investigation it becomes clear that most are untrue or have been altered to such an extent that one cannot distinguish fact from fiction. None of these have been recounted in this book. What we have included is an account of the rigorous selection procedure, the intensive training involved in becoming an operational ranger, examples of national and international deployments, and some of the skills required to operate within this environment.

Along with regular Irish Defence Forces units, the ARW has conducted a number of operational deployments both at home and abroad since its inception, the first in December 1983. Today, The Wing is set to assume an increasing role both nationally and internationally, all the while ensuring that it will continue to be mission ready and adaptable to changing global circumstances.

GENESIS

1

WARS WITHOUT FRONTS

In the aftermath of the Second World War, colonies throughout the world that for centuries had yielded an abundance of materials and wealth to European empires began to grow restless. With many of these empires struggling to rebuild after the war, anti-colonialists began to question and oppose the occupation of their lands by these foreign powers. Peaceful protest soon gave way to violent uprisings and insurgencies in many countries, as nationalist forces fought the colonists. Throughout the 1950s and the early 1960s the world was ablaze with what were to become known as 'Small Wars'. Burma, Indochina, Egypt, Palestine and Algeria were some of the many countries that erupted into violence. In the 1960s, inspired by these uprisings, as well as Mao's Chinese revolution of 1949 and Castro's Cuban revolution of 1953–59, other countries followed suit. In many instances, the fighting disintegrated into bitter guerrilla warfare, with the insurgencies and counter-insurgencies brutal in their extremes.

While the terrain and the customs of those fighting

for their independence varied considerably, one factor that tended to unify each separate conflict was the support of Russia and China for one side and the United States and its allies for the other. The spread of communist doctrine and anti-imperialism enabled Eastern Bloc powers to gain a foothold in countries throughout the world struggling for independence. While the United States disliked colonial rule, their disdain stemming from their own fight for freedom against the British, they initially believed that propping up colonial empires was essential when it came to stemming the socialist tide. As a result, by the late 1960s the Cold War was being fought by proxy in the jungles of South-East Asia, on the plains of Africa and in the mountainous regions of South America.

Alongside this, the post-war generation in America and Western Europe was becoming radicalised, with many openly questioning and protesting their government's involvement in these overseas conflicts. It was during this turbulent period that a number of violent left-wing revolutionary groups and right-wing extremists emerged. Terrorist acts soon followed.

In July 1968 three armed members of the Popular Front for the Liberation of Palestine hijacked El Al Flight 426 as it flew from Rome to Tel Aviv. The plane, with a crew of ten and thirty-eight passengers, was diverted to Algiers by the hijackers, who demanded the release of fellow Palestinians imprisoned in Israel. Forty days of tense negotiations between the hijackers and authorities followed, with the passengers eventually being released unharmed when sixteen Arab prisoners were released. The Palestinian Liberation Organisation's United Nations observer, Zehdi Lahib Terzi, in relation to the seizure of flight 426, is quoted in *The New Yorker* as stating that this hijacking 'awakened the media and public opinion much more … than 20 years of pleading' by the Palestinians.[1]

This terrorist act received a lot of media attention and, as a result, was seen by many other extremist organisations as an effective tool for bringing attention to a cause that would otherwise be ignored by both the media and governments. Other groups quickly emerged, such as the Provisional Irish Republican Army (Ireland), the Weathermen (USA), the Black Panthers (USA), the Symbionese Liberation Army (USA) and the Baader-Meinhof gang (Germany). Within a short period of time, these organisations, and others, turned to violent tactics, from rioting and setting off bombs, to assassinations and hijackings. Weapons and explosives were easily accessible at the time, including modern, compact, rapid-fire submachine guns that were easily concealable. Automatic pistols, manufactured almost entirely of plastic, were easy

---

1   *The New Yorker*, 14 April 1976.

to disassemble and conceal, enabling them to be brought through airport scanners with ease. Targets chosen were more often than not designated 'soft' (i.e. easy to attack), enabling terrorists to inflict maximum damage and casualties. Guerrilla warfare, long thought to be a rural phenomenon, became increasingly urbanised.

Governments throughout the world initially struggled to contain these actions, as many were unprepared for the onslaught of terrorist attacks that occurred from the late 1960s and into the 1970s. At this time, no dedicated counter-terrorist force existed in any European country. Then one terrorist act occurred that would change everything.

On 5 September 1972 Palestinian Black September terrorists broke into the quarters of the Israeli team at the Munich Olympic Village, taking eleven hostages, two of whom were subsequently murdered. The Germans were unprepared for such a situation and their handling of the incident was to have far-reaching repercussions.

Negotiations between the German authorities and the group commenced, with the terrorists demanding the release of a number of their Palestinian associates held in Israeli jails, along with two founders of the Red Army Faction, a far-left militant organisation. They also demanded a chartered flight to Cairo to secure their getaway. After repeated threats by the terrorists against the hostages, the German government informed them that their demands would be met. They would be flown from the Olympic Village to Fürstenfeld Airport, where they would board a Lufthansa flight to Cairo.

However, in reality the German police were planning to neutralise the terrorists at the airfield. Police officers took up positions there, some dressed as air and ground crew, with police marksmen taking up posts overlooking the plane on the runway. All were tasked with killing or capturing the terrorists as they boarded the plane.

As the helicopters carrying the terrorists and their hostages approached the field, some police officers decided that the mission was too risky and stood down, leaving only a five-man team of marksmen to take out the terrorists. Instead of the expected five terrorists accompanying the remaining hostages, the police discovered that there were in fact eight of them. As the terrorists and hostages left the helicopters and approached the plane, the order was given to open fire.

A gunfight commenced, which resulted in the deaths of all the hostages, one policeman and five of the eight terrorists. None of the police marksmen were trained snipers and so they mostly missed their moving targets. Two of the police officers were hit by so-called 'friendly fire'. The operation from start to finish was an unmitigated disaster and a huge embarrassment for the German government. To add salt to the already smarting wounds of Germany, the government was forced to release the surviving terrorists the following month, after a Lufthansa airliner on a flight from Damascus to Frankfurt was hijacked.

In the aftermath of the debacle, the German government took steps to ensure that, in the future, its country would have an effective counter-terrorism response. This decision paved the way for the formation of the first dedicated intervention unit in Europe: the famous Grenzschutzgruppe 9, more commonly referred to as GSG 9.

The French soon followed suit with the formation of GIGN. The British, who had resurrected the Special Air Service (SAS) in the aftermath of the Second World War for the Malayan crisis, directed their 22 SAS (the name of the regular, active-duty regiment of the SAS) to develop a counter-terrorism capability.[2]

While some countries began to organise and counter the increasing terrorist threat, others attempted to appease such groups by succumbing to their demands, paying ransoms and releasing prisoners. This, more often than not, only exacerbated the problem. With terrorist organisations

2   The Malayan Emergency was a guerrilla war fought in the pre- and post-independence Federation of Malaya from 1948 to 1960. British forces fought the National Liberation Army, the military arm of the Malayan Communist Party.

now receiving international recognition through the medium of television, their message was reaching a much larger audience and, for that reason, they were eager to continue with their actions.

Increasingly a new global war was emerging, where new strategies and tactics would have to be devised and deployed. Reconnaissance, counter-terrorism, counter-insurgency and intelligence gathering would be just some of the skills needed by these new units. This new war would be one without fronts, and those operating in this war would have to adapt and overcome numerous obstacles in order to triumph.

2

INCEPTION

Since the formation of the Irish Defence Forces in 1924, the army had been run along conventional lines, similar to other armies throughout the world. Austerity had for decades affected the force, resulting in minimal investment in equipment. However, the Irish Defence Forces' participation in the United Nations missions to Lebanon in 1958 and to the Congo from 1960 to 1964 opened up new horizons. Though overseas service highlighted many shortcomings, these missions enabled the force to work with other armies, use new equipment and recognise their need to adapt.

In 1968 a core training group of officers was chosen to plan and conduct a specialist course to train soldiers for small unit operations. This group included officers from the Military College at the Curragh Camp in Co. Kildare, such as Commandant Eamon Quigley, Captain Des Swan, Captain Jimmy Farrell and Lieutenant Harry Johnson. They were joined by Lieutenants John Vize, Joe Fallon, Des Travers and R. E. M. Heaslip. Initial administrative delays did not deter the soldiers from their mission, and within a short period of time a provisional syllabus had been drawn up, suitable training grounds had been selected, equipment secured and it was ensured that all course instructors were at the peak of their physical prowess. A section from this group was also detailed to undergo specialist training at the United States Army Ranger School located at Fort Benning, Georgia. Those completing this course would then add elements of what they learned to the syllabus for the Irish course.

The US Army Rangers are America's original force of elite soldiers. Their origins date back to the seventeenth- and eighteenth-century wars between colonists and Native American tribes. However, the modern US Army Rangers were actually founded in Ireland, in 1942, during the Second World War. Many US troops were stationed in the North of Ireland at the time, before moving to England. And so it was here, at the behest of Colonel Lucian Truscott, that General George Marshall authorised the establishment of an American unit 'along the lines of the British Commandos'. On 19 June 1942 the 1st Ranger Battalion was sanctioned, recruited and began training in Carrickfergus, Co. Antrim.

In the years that followed, the Rangers were deployed in a number of theatres of war, including Korea and Vietnam. The conflict in Vietnam in particular, which began in 1955, was a precursor of the guerrilla-style insurgencies that have come to define modern combat. Military instructors, many having served in South-East Asia, studied the tactics used against them in the war and developed counter-insurgency measures, as well as working out how to emulate some insurgency actions. The Rangers then incorporated these tactics into their training.

In early 1969 Captain Farrell and Lieutenant Johnson reported to the Ranger Training Brigade at Fort Benning. The purpose of the course they undertook was to train soldiers as combat leaders while they endured great mental and physical stresses. Training was divided into three phases and consisted of precisely 19.6 hours of training each day, to be conducted at three separate geographical locations. Military timing is precise and, after years of running the course, the instructors knew exactly how long they could push the men. Soldiers were trained in a number of general skill sets, including fieldcraft, planning and executing daily patrolling, performing reconnaissance and ambushes, as well as raids against dispersed targets. Training missions simulated the stress that a soldier would feel in combat and in doing so enabled the candidate to plan and organise while becoming inoculated against these pressures. Leadership was an important factor of the training; the participants learned to lead from the front, striking hard and fast.

The course also provided the students with practical experience in the application of the tactics and techniques used in Ranger operations over various terrains, including wooded, lowland swamp and mountainous environments. The candidate was taught how to sustain themselves and their subordinates, and to maintain their equipment under difficult field conditions. Soldiers underwent route marches and combat water survival tests, while the fundamentals of combat operations, including battle techniques, were drilled into them. The men also underwent instruction in advanced mountaineering that included practising survival skills in harsh mountainous terrain. Furthermore, the usual tests of marches with weapon and equipment, as well as day and night navigational skills, were continuously assessed throughout the course. Through all this, it was aimed to further develop the candidate's military skills in the planning and conducting of a variety of operations, including dismounted infantry, airborne, air assault and amphibious squad and platoon-sized combat operations.

The training consisted of an extremely intense programme and the result was an accumulation of physical and mental fatigue that worsened as the course itself became more demanding. This was a deliberate policy to ensure that an individual was tested to see whether or not they had the ability to operate effectively under increasing pressure. It also ensured that only the best made it through selection. The two Irish officers both passed the course.

Back in Ireland, the core group of officers who had been assigned to plan and conduct the course for the Irish Defence Forces encountered a number of setbacks. For example, suitable combat uniforms, ponchos, ration packs, hexamine cookers, abseiling equipment and other kit essential to completing the course were not readily available. The starting date was pushed back, but, undeterred, the men wasted no time in formulating more plans and exercises to be included in the syllabus, some of which had been incorporated from the US Ranger course. And this core group of officers was always looking for fresh ideas.

In March 1969 three other officers of the training team, Lieutenants Fallon, Vize and Travers, made their way to England to participate in a commando course, hoping to glean important training techniques from the experience. This intensive course included a speed march of 6 miles (9.65 kilometres) that had to be completed in sixty minutes. This march was carried out in full kit and finished at a rifle range with a marksmanship test. A second endurance test was carried out over rough terrain and consisted of overcoming obstacles and crawling through tunnels (some filled with water). The time restriction for this test was eighty minutes and finished at the rifle range, where marksmanship was once again tested. The third test consisted of an assault course carried out over varying obstacles, while carrying weapon and kit, and had to be accomplished in five minutes. A 12-mile (19.3-kilometre) cross-country trek carrying 90 pounds (40.8 kilogrammes) of equipment also had to be completed.

In the course of their training, candidates were watched closely and graded not only for their physical fitness and aptitude, but also their attitude and ability to work with others. Under constant scrutiny, their personal qualities, such as professional ability, general conduct, unselfishness and leadership potential, were all graded. One veteran described the course as 'a microcosm of war', since it taught and tested weapons handling and tactical skills, as well as building an individual's stamina and strength.

In June 1969, with the overseas Ranger and commando courses completed, the officers assembled once again at the Military College in the Curragh Camp. Taking on board all that they learned from those experiences, they finalised their new course's comprehensive and demanding programme of training, which would require a high degree of physical fitness and professional knowledge to successfully complete. The course objective, outlined in the syllabus of training at the time, was: 'Using a fighting patrol [a combat group with sufficient strength to raid or ambush an enemy] as a mechanism of instruction, conduct sub-unit level operations in order to improve the personal confidence, leadership, and navigation skills of the officer students.'[1]

In early July 1969 Lt Harry Anderson, 2/Lt Wally Freyne, Lt Jim Murray, 2/Lt Mattie O'Brien, Lt Peter Archibold, 2/Lt Ollie Grey, Lt Brendan McCann, 2/Lt Dan O'Keeffe, 2/Lt Dermot Earley, Lt Tom Hodson, Lt Brian McKevitt and 2/Lt Enda Savage were the first participants to arrive at the Curragh Camp to undertake this demanding specialist training. A new chapter in the history of the Irish Defence Forces was about to commence.

---

1   *Ranger Syllabus of Training* (Irish Defence Forces Printing Press, Dublin, 1969), p. 13.

3

'WE ARE RANGERS'

The dawn chorus at the Curragh Camp was drowned out by the chant, 'We are Rangers, mighty, mighty Rangers.' The group jogged through the barracks grounds, breaking into a sprint, before settling back into a steady pace and then disappearing into the early morning mist.

The twelve officers who had reported for specialist training at the camp were billeted at the Infantry School, with minimal comforts, the sleeping quarters consisting of only mattresses and sleeping bags.

Colonel Dan O'Keeffe (Retd), then a second lieutenant, recalls:

> *I can assure you that what we had in comparison to today's ARW was extremely basic. I remember at the time that the specialist equipment ordered from the UK didn't turn up and the start of the course was delayed.*[1]

---

1   *1st Defence Forces Ranger Course: 40th Anniversary Celebration* (Irish Defence Forces Printing Press, Dublin, 2009), p. 5.

When the course eventually commenced, it was intensive, consisting of eighteen-hour days, with the first week concentrating on technical lessons that covered patrol skills, an introduction to navigation, survival techniques and explosives training.

Colonel Harry Johnson (Retd), then an instructor with the rank of lieutenant, recalls:

> *I suppose at the time it was a completely new kind of concept in the army. All training in our younger days was very formal and straightforward, more marching and minor tactics, and things like that. This was the first time you could get out on the mountains and really challenge you[rself] against the environment. Our equipment allowed you to stay out in the rain or the snow while learning to survive in extreme weather.*[2]

Patrol skills involved candidates learning the importance of negotiating terrain and arriving at the right place at the right time. The military definition of patrolling 'is the means by which a force dominates an area'.[3] Patrolling, especially on foot, is particularly important in certain environments. Therefore, economy of movement, finding suitable routes, the best observation points and the best

---

2   *Ibid.*
3   *Army Ranger Wing – 21st Anniversary Paper* (Irish Defence Forces Printing Press, Dublin, 2001), p. 7.

cover, as well as recognising suitable firing positions that don't expose an individual to enemy fire, were all part of the soldiers' first week of instruction. As the perfect route does not exist, the men were taught to find an acceptable compromise. Making the decision about the best route can mean the difference between a successful mission and one that may end in disaster.

Navigation is an essential technique for ARW operations. Missions can require operatives to travel through unfamiliar terrain consisting of natural and man-made obstacles. The importance of day and night navigational techniques was drilled into the candidates, so that they could find their way to and from their designated destinations. Soldiers were also expected to mount military operations in a variety of inhospitable environments, often at short notice. As a result, the men were instructed on how to manage and survive in extreme weather conditions and different regions, such as mountain areas, deserts, tropical and Arctic environments.

Ranger operations would often require an operative to be in action behind enemy lines and involve the disruption of enemy services, supplies or industrial output by violent means. Explosives and demolition training therefore formed a key element of the instruction, along with the identification of important targets, such as communication centres and command and control networks. Targets are selected according to their strategic and tactical value. Instructors taught the students how to use high explosives and how, in order to set off high explosives, an 'initiator' (a device used to detonate explosives) has to be employed. The two different types, electrical and non-electrical, were used.

During the second week of training, the group moved to Co. Wicklow, where a long-range instructional patrolling exercise was carried out. Three teams were dropped off at various points on the eastern side of the Wicklow Mountains and were tasked to complete navigation, recce (reconnaissance) and liaison tasks en route to a patrol base located at Kavanagh's Gap in the Glen of Imaal. On completion of that patrol, the students were instructed, along with a number of other fighting patrols, to engage the enemy in the area of operations (AO). The primary task of fighting patrols is to harass the enemy, thus lowering its morale. This includes conducting raids to gain intelligence and to capture prisoners for interrogation, carrying out attacks against specific targets, and preventing the enemy from obtaining information about the disposition and strength of friendly forces operating in a particular area.

On completion of these modules the candidates were transported via helicopter to Dún Laoghaire harbour where they underwent water-confidence training. This involved the soldiers jumping from helicopters into the sea. This is an essential skill, given the importance of rapid insertion into a combat zone by different means as quickly and efficiently as possible. It was a key part of the candidate's training.

The third week of training took place across the River Shannon in the wilds of Co. Mayo. Nephin Mountain in North Mayo proved a difficult and arduous location for the candidates. With weapons and full kit, they trekked and climbed the conical-shaped quartzite mountain that overlooks Lough Conn. As the second highest peak in the province of Connaught, the soldiers knew this would be a difficult task. The groups moved off, climbing above the forest to the heather-clad slopes. Rocky outcrops consisting of scree and boulders were traversed and, as they gained height, they encountered cairns. These, in many cases, gave the groups the impression that they had reached the peak, only to then discover another cairn lying ahead. As they approached the summit the gradient got flatter and the underlying surface became stony. Once again, patrolling and survival were key elements being tested during this period of instruction.

During week four, the training moved to South Mayo for further long-range patrolling over the Croagh Patrick mountain range, Partry Mountain and the Devil's Mother. The group exercised in the Tourmakeady Gaeltacht before moving towards and crossing Killary Harbour. Using a local boatman, Festy Mortimer, the patrol embarked from the pier, headed north and landed on the shore under Mweelrea Mountain. The inclement Irish weather, as well as the difficult terrain, made the going tough, but the six-day patrol continued cross-country, reaching its ultimate destination at Louisburg.

Having successfully completed the course, the soldiers returned to the Curragh Camp. Having undertaken one of the most difficult courses to be devised in Ireland's military history at that time, the students and instructors were returned to their respective units with the specialist skills and knowledge that they had mastered. Not only were they now trained in unconventional warfare, but they could also impart some of their knowledge to others within the Defence Forces.

The late Lieutenant General Dermot Early, then a student with the rank of second lieutenant, recalled:

I suppose it was a bit daunting in the sense that we were going into the unknown. We had an idea of what would be required in terms of fitness, but we were unsure of our ability to carry out the tasks the instructors had put in place for us. However, from the training we had already received as cadets we were well capable of bringing our fitness up to the required level and we adapted very quickly to the rolls, tactics, procedures and techniques that were required on the day. Although it was daunting, it was a wonderful experience conducting operations in Wicklow and along the west coast. When it was all over there was a great sense of achievement.[4]

The completion of this first course coincided with the civil rights campaign in the North and the subsequent escalation of violence in that region.

The Defence Forces utilised their newly trained soldiers to run Ranger-type training for officers and non-commissioned officers (NCOs) from all commands. Between late August and early December 1969, officers associated with the first Ranger course stationed in the Military College in the Curragh Camp took on the training of a new intake of soldiers in basic patrolling skills. Over a ten-week period, 300 personnel were trained in small unit patrolling skills. The courses were conducted in appalling weather conditions. Soldiers swapped their 'Bull's Wool' uniforms for waterproof, lightweight British Army surplus combat fatigues.

Brigadier General Jimmy Farrell (Retd), then a captain and an instructor on the course, recalls:

> *There was a great interest from the rest of the Defence Forces in what we were doing, which was very different and challenging from the norm at the time. After the first course it opened up to the rest of the army and there were a huge number of volunteers*

4   *1st Defence Forces Ranger Course: 40th Anniversary Celebration,* p. 9.

with very large courses conducted in the Military College. This,
of course, added to the Defence Forces as a whole. For when more
and more soldiers were trained up, units going overseas were able
to bring these men with them, adding to the resources available
to the commanders.[5]

On completion of these courses, participants were re-turned to their parent units, as there was no dedicated specialist component within the Defence Forces at that time.

Regardless, the instructors and students of the first Defence Forces' Rangers course had established, and would continue, the training and implementation of a special operations capability within the army.

---

5   *Army Ranger Wing – 21st Anniversary Paper,* p. 4.

4

THE SPECIAL ASSAULT GROUP

The carnage caused by the terrorist attack on Israeli athletes at the 1972 Munich Olympics, and the escalating violence in the North of Ireland, made it clear to the Irish government, and other countries throughout the world, that specialist units trained to deal with and counteract these attacks were required as a matter of priority. Terrorist organisations were evolving, with cells using more sophisticated methods and military hardware in their attacks. While the police in Ireland, An Garda Síochána, would continue in their front-line role against terrorism, a dedicated unit with a specialist military capacity was deemed a necessity as an aid to the civil power.

Ranger courses continued throughout the decade that followed the initial course. In the mid-1970s the Defence Forces established a new 'Special Training Course' for selected units for each of its brigades. It was envisaged that, as there was no dedicated specialist group in Ireland to deal with terrorist actions or threats at this time, a chosen contingent in each command throughout the country would be given additional training. This would prepare commands for any situation that they might encounter in their AO. Personnel for these courses were taken from infantry battalions and core units of each command, as well as being selected from amongst all ranks of the army, Air Corps and Naval Service. Given that the course was a welcome change to the spit and polish of daily military life, many soldiers volunteered to take part.

The course was designated the 'Special Assault Group (SAG) Course'. Many of its instructors, such as Commandant R. E. M. Heaslip, Captain Ailbe O'Sullivan and Captain Wally Freyne had participated in the 1969 Ranger course, as well as receiving additional training abroad in the intervening years.

The SAG course was very intensive and conducted over a five-week period in various military locations throughout the country. As the candidates were to be introduced to insurgency and counter-insurgency techniques and skills, the course participants operated in small units, often sections or squads. The importance of map reading and land navigation by day and night was drilled into the soldiers, giving them the required confidence and ability to conduct operations in unfamiliar terrain. This was an essential skill, especially at night, as assault groups would likely be dropped behind enemy lines in the hours of darkness to carry out their missions.

In Co. Cork, training exercises were carried out in Kilworth, as well as on the Galtee Mountains range spread across Counties Limerick and Tipperary. The programme consisted of early morning physical training (PT) runs, fieldcraft, unarmed combat, methods of deployment from vehicles and small arms training. Respirator drills, helicopter drills and classes in demolition were also conducted. Course participants were subjected to high levels of PT through obstacle courses that were specially constructed to test their agility and speed.

Combat and survival training comprised an intensive course of instruction and tests in all aspects of surviving as an effective soldier in a hostile environment. The basic elements of the survival training programme included the building of a shelter, finding food and water, laying traps for small game and making fire.

Candidates also practised the relevant offensive and defensive patrolling tactics, as well as manoeuvres designed to get them to think outside the box. Standard operating procedures (SOPs), as they are referred to, include movement through hostile territory, contact drills and learning the arcs of fire of each patrol member. In a patrol, when it comes to the arcs of fire, each soldier is assigned a specific role – and therefore arc. When moving in file, the leading man covers the area to the front of the patrol in the arc between ten and two o'clock, the man behind him covers the arc between six and ten o'clock or between two to six o'clock, the third man covers the opposite arc to the man in front of him and the fourth man covers the rear of the patrol.

Further patrol actions included route selection, patrol discipline, fieldcraft, navigation by day and night, as well as actions on rendezvous, forward rendezvous (FRV) and escape rendezvous (ERV). The use of 'comms' (communication devices) and other 'actions on' objectives were also tested.

It was imperative that the SOPs became second nature to the candidates, so that their trained actions could ensure the survival of the patrol. Therefore, team members were taught and encouraged to make decisions, take control and become an effective junior leader in all types of patrolling operations.

Marksmanship was also tested with live-fire training exercises. Soldiers fired from a static position at pop-up targets, as well as on the move. This was carried out individually and as part of a section (i.e. group of soldiers). Students were given realistic combat scenarios through the use of live ammunition with different section and platoon weapons. These exercises were carried out during the day and at night. They also trained in advanced weapon skills, and by the end of the course were familiar with all section weapons.

Soldiers were taught how to conduct military operations in urban terrain (MOUT). This consisted of offensive and defensive operations, urban concealment, as well as fire and movement in this difficult operational environment. They were also monitored for stability under stress, with instructors looking for an individual's confidence in their ability to conduct a patrol and whether they could lead by example.

At this time, specialist units throughout the world were concentrating on hostage-rescue tactics, with precision training assaults on planes, trains and buildings. As a result, the SAG had to adapt and improvise. Liaising with the special forces community throughout the world, the SAG instructors participated in information exchanges with their counterparts. This gave the Irish Defence Forces a broader knowledge of the subject. Utilising basic equipment, through trial and error the SAG devised new strategies and tactics that gave soldiers the skills and means to assist the civil power in these situations if needed.

The attributes demanded of a SAG operative included strong motivation and full commitment; a good personality and complete integrity; the ability to think, both logically and laterally; organisational skill; adaptability; confidence; decisiveness; intelligence; and common sense. Though SAG operatives worked in teams, with an emphasis on teamwork, each unit had its dedicated specialists – such as medical, explosives and communications – who, when called upon, could conduct a variety of solo tasks in the field.

Each course provided, in each command, forty Rangers trained in all arms, engineering and ordnance techniques. Within a short period of time, the Defence Forces had 300 operatives throughout the country who could conduct special support operations at the request of An Garda Síochána.

5

THE ARMY RANGER WING

A wave of bombings, killings and kidnappings were carried out in Ireland by insurgent groups in the 1970s. Public houses, town centres and military bases were bombed by loyalists and republicans. In an attempt to help fund their campaigns, prominent businessmen, such as Don Tidey and Tiede Herrema, were kidnapped and held for ransom. Many deaths were caused by improvised explosive devices (IEDs), such as that of the queen's cousin, Lord Louis Mountbatten, and three others when Mountbatten's boat was targeted by the PIRA. This increase in terrorism on the island convinced the government and military planners that a designated unit was needed to counteract the escalating terrorist actions.

In 1978 a presentation paper on international terrorism by Intelligence Section Army Headquarters (Int. Sec. AHQ) identifying the threats to the country – primarily republican and loyalist subversives at the time – submitted recommendations in relation to the establishment of a specialist unit. In the months that followed, the chief of staff carried out a feasibility study in relation to costings, personnel, training and the equipment required for the establishment of a new unit.

In 1979 the foundation of the Irish ARW was sanctioned by the Department of Defence. This was followed by the appointment of an officer commanding (O/C) and second-in-command (2 I/C). The appointment of the first O/C of the ARW took place on 16 March 1980. Commandant (later Colonel) R. E. M. Heaslip (Retd) was given the task of establishing and forming the unit. (Captain Wally Freyne completed both the selection and skills course and in 1982 became 2 I/C of the ARW.)

A base for the unit was established in the 'Jail Centre' complex in the Curragh Camp and, soon after, the first selection and training courses were initiated. The ARW was to be held in readiness 24/7, 365 days a year. Its commanding officer was responsible for the unit and it was directly under the command of Army Operations.

The unit was officially designated 'Sciathán Fianóglach an Airm', which is translated as 'The Army Ranger Wing' (there is no direct translation of Fianóglach). On the completion and passing of the selection process, the successful candidates received their shoulder tab with the word Fianóglach on it. This word links the unit to the traditions of the elite and legendary Irish warriors of 'Na Fianna'. The tab was based on the US Ranger flash and was produced by instructors on the first Defence Forces' Ranger course. A red border on the tab was introduced in November 1980 to distinguish serving ARW operatives from other Defence Forces personnel who had completed command Ranger courses.

Once the unit was officially established, the founding members were tasked with putting together the specialist force. Candidates applied from all branches of the Defence Forces, with the course facilitators seeking a high level of physical fitness, navigation skills, personal stamina and, above all, the aspiration to serve in what was to become one of the world's most elite forces. Those applying for selection were stripped of whatever rank and privilege they were accustomed to, with all potential recruits endeavouring to prove that they could stay the length of the selection course. This practice continues to the present day. One ARW operative later recalled the introduction at the training course:

'You are now Rangers of selection course "Uniform" (28/2/88), your soul may belong to God or whoever else you believe in, but for the next four weeks your minds and bodies belong to the Army Ranger Wing.' A selection course student, we were told, is a creature with no rank except Ranger and as such we addressed everything that walked upright on two legs in the Curragh as 'D.S. [Directing Staff]'.[1]

1 'Expect the Unexpected', *An Cosantóir*, July 1988, p. 34.

For the selection course, instructors utilised the original specialist unit training syllabus, as well as adding components to cover the rapidly changing international military arena. Candidates were assessed and evaluated on their physical fitness, motivation and suitability through a series of tests that included fitness assessments, map reading, water confidence and psychometric evaluation (measuring a person's mental capabilities).[2] In order to progress, candidates were assessed further by a series of individual navigation exercises that required the candidates to march up to 60 kilometres cross-country, carrying a 65-pound combat load. A footnote at the end of the Joining Instructions gave a hint that only the foolhardy ignored – if you bring it, you carry it.

Each day consisted of sixteen to twenty-one hours of extensive lectures, demonstrations and tutorials. Outside the classroom environment, candidates were subjected to a number of confidence tests.

Standing on the 115-foot-high water tower in the Curragh Camp, Captain (later Commandant) Traolach Sweeney, an accomplished mountaineer, instructed the candidates in the skill of abseiling. Those who baulked at the test were told that they did not have to participate and that they could avail of the get-out clause known as

---

2   An examination component was added in 2015.

'RTU' (Returned To Unit, i.e. failing the course and being returned to your unit).

The water confidence test was just as daunting as the height test. Candidates were transported from Dún Laoghaire harbour out to the Irish Sea by the Naval Service. There, the men had to jump off the ship dressed in their full combat uniforms. Having landed in the water they had to swim back to the ship and scramble up the net hanging from the side of the vessel and jump off again, but this time from a higher level.

Another test involved candidates being taken a considerable distance from the ship in a Rigid Inflatable Boat (RIB) where they were then ordered to jump overboard and swim back to the vessel. The weight of their water-laden uniforms, the cold of the water and distance back to the ship tested the men's skills and stamina to their limits.

Weapons training on the course was paramount, with students spending hours stripping, assembling and firing numerous types and calibres of firearms. Remaining tests examined weapons skills through marksmanship. One selection course student recalled:

> *A Ranger never left his weapon out of his hands as the ARW staffs were always on the prowl trying to acquire one. Loss of a weapon, even for ten seconds, meant instant dismissal from the course so that*

the FN [Fabrique Nationale] Rifle accompanied you to meals, bed and even into the shower.[3]

Failure to have your weapon with you at all times resulted in a candidate being RTU'ed.

The first selection course also consisted of an 'escape and evasion' exercise. This took place on Bere Island, located off the Beara peninsula in Co. Cork. The island covers 17.68 square kilometres, with an elevation of 270 metres. Assaulting the island, candidates were tasked with launching an attack on a heavily defended facility. They were repulsed (by soldiers from local Defence Forces units supported by the Rangers in charge) and subsequently captured. The prisoners were disarmed, searched and stripped of all their equipment. They were then held in a disused fort on the island that was lightly guarded, allowing them to escape. Having gained their freedom, they had to evade capture for as long as possible. With their survival skills they had to live off the land, avoiding contact with the local population, if possible, as well as evading specialist search teams sent out to track them down.

At the end of the exercise, all those who had evaded capture had to 'surrender' themselves to the main force

---

3   'Expect the Unexpected', *An Cosantóir*, July 1988, p. 34.

and were then moved to an interrogation centre where they underwent perhaps the most mentally gruelling part of an ARW soldier's training – the twenty-four-hour resistance to interrogation exercise. Throughout this exercise, the soldier is subjected to extremes of both mental and physical stress, through sleep deprivation, intensive questioning and humiliation. This part of the course is designed to see if the candidate can be made to yield information beyond the permitted maximum of name, rank and number.

For the remaining participants, the second main section of the course involved long-range patrolling in mountainous terrain. Working both in small numbers and independently, groups and individuals trekked across inhospitable terrain, conducting hit-and-run missions against an unseen enemy who never seemed to let up in their pursuit of the Rangers:

> *Each individual was tested on his ability to navigate, to conduct patrols, to carry out assaults on enemy positions and to organise new base camps. The day to day activity was basically – break camp, mountain patrol to new location, make agent contact, assault enemy position, establish new base camp and then move to new base camp site with pre-recced assault on enemy location. These activities were not just limited to day-light hours.*[4]

---

4   *Ibid.*

However, it was the final week that proved the most arduous for the recruits. After hours of night marches, candidates had to finish the week by conducting a 40-kilometre route march that ended at the Curragh Camp. One ARW candidate said of this final test:

> *The feeling was that if we had made it so far, we could make it the rest of the way, thus morale and determination were very high. The warm and unexpected welcome by the OC and staff of the Ranger Wing at the gates of the ARW HQ made it all worthwhile and gave everyone a great feeling of pride.*[5]

On completion of the selection course, students were attached to the ARW unit for a further six-month assessment period. Those that proved unsuitable after this period were returned to their old units.

---

5   *Ibid.*

6

TRIAL AND ERROR

For those who completed the selection course, training continued unabated. The soldiers received instruction in direct action, special reconnaissance and surveillance, and military assistance techniques. Defensive operations included the protection of VIPs, counter-insurgency, and the conduct of specialist and delay operations. Given that the purpose of the unit was to take on a counter-terrorism role, training also included conducting counter-hijack operations, hostage rescue, airborne and seaborne interventions, search missions, pursuit, re-capture of terrorist-held objectives, close protection, and contingency planning to counteract planned terrorist or subversive threats.

With no dedicated budget for the unit, requests for financial support and specialist equipment had to be put through the system and followed up. This often caused delays, and in many cases the ARW staff had to improvise, adapt and overcome.

When it came to the uniform, the operatives wore the

army-issue plain green combats and boots, although some soldiers preferred to purchase Alpine hiking boots instead of accepting the poor-quality standard-issue boots. Unit members wore a brassard (armband) on their upper left arm with their Fianóglach tab with a red border to distinguish them from other army units. Specialist kit was not available. The unit's standard first man pack (backpack) was made by Lowe Alpine. This was plain green in colour with a detachable padded belt which became a soldier's operational belt. It consisted of two pocket pouches in the front with an attachment for a holster. The belt could also be converted into a climbing harness for abseiling. The distinctive green beret awarded to an ARW operative when they become part of the unit was introduced later, in 1986.

Once up and running, the ARW worked closely with other units within the Irish Defence Forces in order to improve their skill set. A vital requirement for ARW operatives was to be able to clandestinely infiltrate and exfiltrate target areas rapidly. Insertion by air, specifically by parachute, was one such highlighted skill. The Army Parachute Club, founded in 1972 by Commandant Con McNamara, would receive The Wing's first candidates for jumping. The soldiers underwent a basic static-line course. (A static line is a fixed cord attached to a large stable object. It is used to open parachutes automatically for parachutists, as well as novice parachutists.) This gave the Rangers the necessary skills required. Following the completion of the course, which was conducted in conjunction with the Air Corps, they received the coveted parachute wings.

The ARW also worked closely with the Irish Naval Service in relation to insertion by water. The first ARW combat divers course was conducted by the Naval Service in June 1983. By 1989 the unit was training using a combat rubber raiding craft (CRRC).

Having undergone all this additional training and achieving the high standard of an ARW operator, a soldier was then posted to an operational ARW assault platoon as an assault team operator.

On the unit's formation, the ARW found itself having to adapt to a variety of functions. Its tasks included conventional warfare, as well as the implementation of a new role to counteract the acts of terror that were being perpetrated by terrorist organisations. On 4 December 1981 two ARW soldiers, Commandant T. Sweeney and Lieutenant G. O'Leary, were sent abroad to take part in an Anti-Terrorist Intervention Course conducted by the GIGN in Maisons-Alfort, Paris, France. This course, run over a number of weeks, saw the ARW take on its 'Black Role' (aid to the civil power, which included a counter-terrorism function), as the two officers who had taken part in the course returned and instructed others in the relevant skills. Following on from this, black tracksuits were acquired and used during training.

Those commanding the unit were tasked with establishing and exploring the CT tactics, training and technology needed to defeat the threats Ireland now faced from numerous terrorist groups. Black and green roles were devised to differentiate between CT and other tasks required from the ARW. The green role was one of conventional warfare that included long-range patrolling, special reconnaissance and direct action missions. The black was CT.

Of course, it is only when negotiations with terrorists break down that an assault becomes necessary, and the preferred method to end a hostage situation is always one of arbitration. However, in many cases the only way to ensure the safety of hostages is to eliminate the threat by force. ARW operatives were therefore trained in sustained and accurate shooting, using a variety of firearms. Weapons on general issue to the Irish Defence Forces were deemed unsuitable for CT operations and so new weapons, more suitable for close-quarter combat, were tried and tested. Weapons manufactured by the German company Heckler & Koch proved suitable and reliable. These became the weapons of choice of special forces units around the world, and they were deemed innovative for their design and manufacture, such as the use of lightweight polymers and the integral rail used to place flashlights on weapons. The American companies, Browning, and Smith and Wesson, also supplied weapons.

Operatives honed their marksmanship in training, often while breaching entries into planes or buildings within strict time constraints. The emphasis on close quarter battle (CQB) skills and room clearances meant the utilisation of buildings at the Jail Centre and elsewhere as 'kill houses'. These exercises tested the operative's technical and practical knowledge to their limits. The buildings comprised a sophisticated series of indoor ranges designed to mirror any conceivable interior that operatives might encounter during an actual hostage rescue mission. Structures that were used for these training operations ranged from semi-detached, two-storey dwellings to multi-roomed government-style complexes, as well as railway carriages and different makes of aircraft and ships.

The operatives were faced with different scenarios and had to adapt rapidly to each one. Often they were confronted with remotely operated, spring-loaded targets representing both hostages and their captors. These were arranged throughout a building or aircraft and set to pop up, to be rescued or engaged. Time and time again the operatives went through these drills, firing thousands of rounds of live ammunition, perfecting their rescue tactics.

These exercises helped develop extraordinarily rapid reflexes and the uncanny ability to appraise the immediate tactical situation within a split second. Pyrotechnic devices, specially adapted vehicles, fast-rope skills and weapon drills were also used and perfected. Specially constructed frame charges, containing explosive charges in strip form, gave the operatives rapid access to a building. These were used to blow precision holes through walls, steel and reinforced glass, as well as windows and doors. Cutting equipment, such as acetylene torches, was also utilised to cut through bars in these training scenarios.

Operatives from that time recount how much of their training was trial and error. 'Scenarios were planned and then carried out using different techniques. If it worked, great. If it didn't, it was back to the drawing board.'[1]

Within a short period of time, the ARW had become a formidable force within the Irish Defence Forces. The continuous training and calibre of those within its ranks made it a force to be reckoned with.

The ARW also began collating information and compiling a comprehensive database to assist its operatives in their CT operations. The information consisted of the thickness and materials of doors, various locking systems, designs of trains and aircraft, and the plans of buildings

---

1 Interview with ARW operative, identity classified.

and complexes throughout the country that may be seen as potential terrorist targets.

In conducting a CT operation, speed and momentum are of the utmost importance. This has not changed greatly from the early days of the ARW. With negotiations severed, the ARW will move into action. The success of the operation will depend on speed and coordination, with the assault teams entering the building simultaneously. If the situation requires a hostage rescue, the teams of operatives will assault the designated target building from above and below. Kitted out in their specialist clothing, and carrying a range of weapons and tools, the units will form up and wait for the signal to go. Utilising frame charges specially designed for use by military forces on fortified bunker doors, a breach or breaches will enable each team to enter the building. Distraction techniques will be used to disorientate the terrorists and give the assault teams an advantage. Once inside, each team and each operative rapidly and systematically begins to clear the rooms, hallways and stairs of enemy personnel, as well as ensuring the safety of the hostages. Room clearance drills, perfected in the 'kill house', are a fast and effective method of securing a building. If doors are locked or barred, one member of the team will blow the door off its hinges or kick it in, while a second operative will toss in stun grenades, or 'flash bangs' as they are more commonly known. Another operative will then follow through, killing any hostile with a double tap or three-round burst from his weapon and at the same time ensuring the safety of any hostage within that space. This action lasts less than four seconds.

ARW training is intense and the men know that the most well-rehearsed of plans can go wrong and that the unit must always allow for the unexpected and meet that challenge head on.

7

AID TO THE CIVIL POWER

As with all units within the Irish Defence Forces, the ARW was given the role of being an aid to the civil power. In practice, this meant that they were to assist, when requested, An Garda Síochána, who have the primary responsibility of upholding law and order in the country, including the protection of the internal security of the state.

Since the formation of the state in 1922, the army has only appeared occasionally with the gardaí, its presence a reassurance to the population that all was well while underlining that all matters of law and order still came under the guise of local policing.

During the early 1970s, however, as paramilitary violence escalated in Ireland, police forces north and south of the border struggled to cope. The response to the crimes perpetrated by the various paramilitary organisations was tentative and initially based on the premise of logical incrementalism, which meant using what was already available – i.e. the expertise of members of the police and the military who were generally to the forefront of the operational activities – and gradually building upon that through additional training.

In the case of An Garda Síochána, this was the unit known as the 'Special Branch' (more properly entitled the 'Special Detective Unit'), which was based at Dublin Castle. Formed in 1922 as the Criminal Investigation Department (CID), this armed group dealt with the paramilitary threat on an ongoing basis, responding to a number of incidents throughout the country.

At first, the ARW was not called upon to assist the gardaí during paramilitary incidents and, according to some, was not even considered for such tasks. Former Assistant Commissioner of An Garda Síochána Thomas C. King wrote:

> While it may have seemed to the Rangers that there was a conspiracy at higher levels of the Garda force not to involve them in operations, the truth was that there was a mixture of a lack of appreciation of the capacity and skills of the Rangers coupled to a certain inevitable 'Go it alone' policy. The attitudes changed in 1981 with the arrival at Garda Headquarters of members and officers who had themselves been involved in the resolution of many spectacular armed incidents, including kidnappings. Despite the success of these operations, those of us who had been directly involved were keenly aware of our shortcomings in terms of equipment, training and appropriate skills.

We were convinced that these skills were available to us at very short notice by a simple request to the army to provide a unit of the Army Ranger Wing.[1]

Subsequent meetings between police officials and ARW commanders resulted in the understanding that both sides would benefit from increased interaction. While certain incidents could be handled by the gardaí, there were others that could only be resolved by the deployment of the ARW. This firmly established the role of the ARW as an aid to the civil power.

From that point on, garda operational planning for major incidents took into account the capacity and availability of the ARW. Pre-planning conferences were held to ensure that the Rangers were adequately informed and briefed, so that, in the event of them being called into action, they already had the information to hand that would enable them to operate with full knowledge of all aspects of the operation.

By the mid-1980s acts of violence were a daily occurrence in Northern Ireland. At the same time, the Irish economy was in an appalling state, with mass unemployment and emigration affecting many families. Large-scale protests, both political and social, were in some cases fol-

---

1   *Army Ranger Wing: 21st Anniversary Paper*, p. 31.

lowed by civil disorder. While the threat posed by subversive groups during this period is well known, the ARW was involved in a number of other operations against less obvious targets.

For example, prison riots in the 1990s, particularly in Mountjoy and Portlaoise prisons, witnessed the deployment of the ARW in support of the police. In 1997 three prisoners armed with knives took two prison officers hostage and barricaded themselves into the medical wing at Mountjoy. As they were threatening to kill the officers, two teams of twelve Rangers took up position and prepared to breach an entry by blowing the steel door into the wing. The aim was to rescue the hostages and eliminate the threat posed by the hostage-takers. However, the siege ended peacefully when, through negotiations, the hostage-takers were informed that the ARW had been deployed. The mere threat of the Rangers was enough to bring an end to the situation.

The ARW was also, potentially, on hand to resolve other tensions. For example, the Irish government is tasked with providing a fishery protection service in accordance with the state's obligations as a member of the European Union. Industrial action by those involved in the fishing industry in the late 1980s threatened the closure of ports throughout the country. If the need arose, the unit was available to clear the blockade, enabling the ports to reopen. However, both sides entered talks and the situation was diffused peacefully.

Overall, however, the ARW does not have a specific role in such operations or in any civil disorder situation unless they are called upon to assist the civil power. The decision to use the ARW in such situations depends on the Taoiseach, who is advised on the capabilities of The Wing by senior security advisers, as well as the ministers for defence and for justice. The military are not permitted to conduct any official armed actions outside their barracks without being under the direct supervision of the civilian authorities. However, the ARW train continuously with the gardaí, simulating various situations, such as kidnappings and hijacking, thereby preparing both forces for working together to ensure a successful outcome in future incidents.

An ARW selection course advert that appeared in *An Cosantóir* magazine in 1988.

All images in this section are courtesy of the Army Ranger Wing and the Defence Forces Public Relations Branch.

Army Ranger Wing
Would You Like To Be A Ranger?

Your training would involve:
- Attaining a high level of fitness, endurance and stamina.
- Advanced weapon handling.
- Marksmanship.
- Combat survival training.
- Parachute training.
- Diving and underwater skills.
- Small boat handling.
- Mountaineering.
- Air — Sea confidence training.

SELECTION COURSE 1988
Selection Course 'UNIFORM' will commence on February 28th, 1988. This will be the only opportunity in 1988 for you to join this specialist unit. Read the conditions for candidates and if the challenge appeals to you apply to undergo the Selection Course. Army Ranger Wing personnel will visit barracks throughout the Defence Forces from mid January to mid February 1988. Avail of this opportunity to discuss service in the Wing with these personnel. We promise you it will NOT be easy to succeed but unless you apply you will never wear the 'GREEN BERET' of the Army Ranger Wing.

Closing date for applications to EPS is Thursday, 18 February, 1988.
Interviews: Officers, Monday, 22 Feb, 1988; Other Ranks, Wednesday, 24 Feb, 1988.

THIS COULD BE YOU!

Are _You_ INTERESTED?

CONDITIONS FOR CANDIDATES

1. Volunteers from any Corps or Service in the PDF.
2. Of a rank NOT less than 3 Star or equivalent.
3. In good physical condition.
4. Medical category A1, with good medical record.
5. In possession of an acceptable Conduct Sheet.
6. Prepared to reside within an approved radius of the Curragh Camp if married.
7. Prepared to give a minimum of 18 months commitment to the Unit.
8. Recommended by his Commanding Officer.

ARW operatives carrying out a counter-terrorist (black) role in the early 1980s.

The ARW conducting counter-terrorist assault training on
the staff house in the Curragh Camp in the early 1980s.

ARW selection course students undergoing conditioning
training on the Curragh Plains *circa* 2004/2005.

An ARW operative conducting counter-terrorism training in the 'kill house' in the ARW compound at the Curragh Camp in 2016.

An ARW team conducting counter-terrorism assault training on a ferry in the Irish Sea in 2011.

ARW and Air Corps combined services conducting counter-terrorism assault training in the military training facility in the Curragh Camp in 2014.

The ARW Special Operations Maritime Task Unit (SOMTU) conducting boarding drills in the naval base, Haulbowline in 2016.

The ARW Maritime Task Unit conducting boarding drills on a Naval Service vessel armed with HK416 assault rifles in 2016.

Part of the ARW initial entry force on patrol in a special reconnaissance vehicle in EUFOR Chad/CAR in 2008.

An ARW patrol operating in Liberia with UNMIL, awaiting extraction by a UN Mi-26 helicopter after a long-range patrol *circa* 2003/2004.

A weapon-mounted system used by an ARW patrol in Liberia *circa* 2003/2004.

An ARW patrol mounting up while awaiting deployment by a New Zealand Huey helicopter in East Timor *circa* 1999/2000.

An ARW sniper team deployed with an Accuracy International .338 rifle and a MOD A3 Steyr rifle with short barrel in Chad in 2008.

The current ARW badges/insignia: (top, l–r) combat divers badge, Ireland flash, sniper qualification badge; (middle) Fianóglach tab with red piping to identify serving or former ARW unit members; (bottom, l–r) subdued para wings for DPM uniform, ARW unit flash and para wings for service dress uniform.

An ARW student receiving his Fianóglach tab on passing the Special Operations Force Qualification Course Module 3 in 2013.

8

THE LONG WAR

In the aftermath of the 1969 civil rights marches, the situation in the North of Ireland deteriorated rapidly, with widespread violence throughout the six counties. British troops were deployed, clashing with both nationalists and loyalists. The Provisional Irish Republican Army (PIRA) and the Ulster Volunteer Force (UVF), as well as other splinter groups, began campaigns of terror with daily bombings and shootings.

In response, the Irish government deployed troops and medical teams along the border to assist refugees fleeing the violence in the North. The government also made it clear that it did not support paramilitary organisations which used violence to achieve their aims. An Garda Síochána established the 'Armed Intervention Unit', tasked with combating subversive groups along the border. This worked closely with the Irish Defence Forces and their counterparts north of the border to stop terrorist attacks and bring those responsible to justice.

In order to fund their activities, the insurgent groups

became adept throughout the 1970s and into the 1980s at raising money through extortion, kidnapping, racketeering and other illegal activities that took place on both sides of the border. It was during one of these activities by the IRA that the ARW conducted its first operation.

The kidnapping of the prominent businessman Don Tidey occurred in Dublin in late 1983 and resulted in the fledgling ARW being deployed. Tidey, a supermarket executive, had been snatched as he drove his thirteen-year-old daughter to school on 24 November. A ransom of IR£5,000,000 was demanded by his kidnappers. A massive manhunt was launched by the gardaí with the army in support. The police tracked Tidey and his kidnappers to a dugout in a secluded woodland in Ballinamore, Co. Leitrim, on 16 December. In the subsequent shoot-out between the kidnappers and Irish security forces, a trainee garda, Gary Sheehan, and an Irish Army soldier, Patrick Kelly, were shot and killed. Tidey was ultimately rescued after twenty-three days in captivity, but the kidnappers escaped.

The ARW was called in after the fatal shoot-out. Moving from its base in the Curragh, the unit was used as a 'Quick Reaction Force' (QRF), providing over-watch (support/cover fire), search teams and stop gaps (taking on the other group's tasks as a temporary measure). Although the ARW was not directly involved in the rescue of

Tidey, lessons were still learned from this operation. For example, it was acknowledged that the police and military needed to work more cohesively in instances like this. The operation ultimately resulted in the police and military refining their tactics and procedures for future operations.

Having received extensive funding from overseas since the 1970s, the IRA was able to procure weapons from international arms dealers and foreign countries, including Libya. Muammar Gaddafi, who seized power in Libya through a coup in 1969, saw the IRA as a comrade in arms fighting British imperialism, and he was partly responsible for providing modern weaponry to the organisation. Heavy and light machine guns, ammunition, explosives and RPG rocket launchers were landed in Ireland and distributed to republican units. Weapons were hidden in caches north and south of the border, to be distributed before an attack and then returned afterwards. British security forces were often frustrated in their attempts to apprehend those responsible for attacks north of the border, as the IRA men, having launched their attack, would often make their escape across the border, hiding their weapons and disappearing in amongst the civilian population.

Aware of these tactics, the ARW was often tasked with surveillance of and intelligence gathering on IRA units based in Ireland. Small teams were used to gather intelligence and relay this information back to headquarters (HQ). Gathering military intelligence, either from static observation posts (OPs) or mobile reconnaissance patrols, was a major part of the ARW's role during this period. The unit was expert in the selection, construction and manning of covert OPs against subversive groups. The location of these could range from an urban to a rural environment and, in many cases, was to be found in inhospitable landscapes. The ARW was deployed along the border and to various locations throughout the country to monitor 'high value targets' and locate and monitor arms caches. Once in position, comms were established with the ARW base, enabling vital intelligence to be passed on to the relevant authorities.

For intelligence-gathering purposes, units were equipped with a special purpose kit, which contained a wide range of equipment, such as binoculars, spotting scopes and night-vision aids. These would be blacked out so as not to reflect the light and therefore not compromise the position of the 'hide'. While 'hides' in rural areas were usually dug out from the earth or secreted in dense woodland, urban OPs ranged from unmarked vehicles to abandoned or derelict buildings.

A number of these covert operations were carried out during the Troubles, with vital intelligence subsequently being passed on to the civil authorities. Arms caches were uncovered and destroyed, as well as key players in the PIRA and Irish National Liberation Army (INLA) being apprehended. They received lengthy prison sentences, ranging from five to forty years, resulting in many serious terrorists being taken out of the equation and, therefore, many lives being saved.

With the signing of the Good Friday Agreement on 10 April 1998, hostilities between warring factions in the North ceased and all sides entered into dialogue. However, the emergence of various splinter groups with the declared intention of destroying the peace process has seen the ARW remain on alert. The unit has proven itself a force to be reckoned with and continues to be an integral factor in ensuring that the peace established in the 1990s survives into the future.

LAND, SEA AND EVERYWHERE

9

THE ARW OVERSEAS

Since 26 June 1958 the Irish Defence Forces have been involved extensively in United Nations (UN) peacekeeping missions throughout the world. To date, Irish military personnel have completed an estimated 70,000 individual tours of duty on peacekeeping operations. In 2018 the Irish Defence Forces celebrated the sixtieth anniversary of their unbroken involvement with UN peacekeeping, and acknowledged the fortieth year of operations with the United Nations Interim Force in Lebanon (UNIFIL).

Following the Israeli invasion of Lebanon in 1978, UNIFIL was established to supervise the withdrawal of Israeli forces and restore peace and security in the region. The Irish Defence Forces were stationed in Tibnin, with an AO that covered an estimated 100 square kilometres. As well as securing the area through patrols and checkpoints, the Irish contingent also provided humanitarian assistance to the local populace. They carried out their duties until 2001, when Israeli forces withdrew from South Lebanon (though a small number of UNIFIL 'observers' remained behind, meaning that they were still technically on the ground). However, in 2006 tensions rose in the region and Irish soldiers were once again deployed in force to the country to carry out peacekeeping duties.

The ARW has often featured on these peacekeeping missions, both in Lebanon and elsewhere. One of its central and most common roles is being tasked with providing 'close protection' (CP), or body-guarding, for a variety of VIPs that include taoisigh, ministers and military personnel who have travelled to the region. The unit conducts two types of CP operations:

1. Long-term CP is conducted when a high-ranking Irish general takes up a high-profile appointment overseas. These types of operations can run for up to two years.

2. Short-term missions are conducted when a taoiseach, minister for defence or chief of staff visits an environment where it is deemed that a close protection team (CPT) is needed for their security. This often entails the team travelling to the location in advance to carry out the planning and preparation work required to ensure the safety of the principals on their visit.

The majority of CP work carried out by the ARW is low-key. The CPT needs to assess the level of overt or covert protection that will be given to the VIP/principal. The unit maintains a safe environment for the principal that allows him/her to carry on with their day-to-day activities without being restricted by the CPT. The principals should be able to interact with the public safely but remain at all times under the CP safety net.

In order to determine the level of safety required for the principal, the CPT must take into account the operating environment, the principal's requirements and the threat level. These can change from day to day or, when in the field, on an hour-to-hour basis, depending on the situation. At all times the team leader (TL) must examine all the factors and implement the solution that will best suit all parties involved. The priority for the TL is the principal's safety at all times.

CP is a 24/7 job and entails a very long and hard day. Some consider this type of mission to be tedious and mundane, but operators must remain focused and alert. Any venue that the principal is visiting must be checked and secured beforehand. A detailed plan of the building must be studied and emergency exits and rendezvous points must be highlighted to all members of the team before they travel with the principal. Detailed security plans will be implemented, taking into account – whenever possible – the people he/she will meet. Route reconnaissance is also carried out by members of the team, looking for potential ambush sites, traffic bottlenecks and choke points, such as roundabouts. A team of eight to twelve operators is required for ARW CP missions.

The kit needed to conduct CP is varied and includes a complete medical bag to deal with the principal's health. Each principal is given a medical checklist to complete so that the CP medic can assess if specialist medication or equipment needs to be carried. Their age, allergies they may have and general health must also be considered by the CPT.

Individual kit depends on the person's role in the CPT, but the basic equipment carried by each member on their person consists of a SIG Sauer P226 pistol with spare magazines, an ASP (retractable baton), a torch, an encrypted team radio for communications from vehicle to vehicle, spare batteries, a mobile phone, a small medical kit and a foldable knife. Grab bags are carried in the vehicles and include spare ammunition, batteries, a medical kit, night vision goggles (NVG) and infra-red strobe lights (IR).

Firepower is used as a last resort. However, if the need arises, the HK416 (5.56 calibre) with a number of enhanced attachments is available. These weapons, carried in the vehicles, enable the team to engage targets at a greater range and with more firepower if the need arises. Depending on the situation, the weapons can also be carried overtly.

Other kit that is deemed essential to CP operations,

such as body armour, respirators in case of a tear-gas attack, breakdown kit for vehicles, water, food and battery packs, are usually carried in the team's vehicles when in covert mode. Possessing the right equipment for the task is essential for the smooth operation of all CP missions.

For the majority of operations little will happen due to the fact that the CPT is doing its job correctly or the principal is not under threat. However, the CPT needs to be constantly on the lookout for any suspicious activities. The ARW has been trained to deal with and counteract any potential threat, ranging from lone attackers to an ambush. There are immediate action drills for any given situation, referred to as 'Reaction to Attack' (RTA), which allow operators to react with speed, power and accuracy. These are able to be implemented without delay in order to bring the situation under control as quickly as possible. For example, if a team is ambushed en route, it will attempt to drive through the 'kill zone'. However, if this is not possible, the team must stop and engage the attackers, protecting the principal while trying to find an alternative route of egress (way to get out).

One of the key attributes the operator possesses is their flexibility. There are a number of different scenarios and environments the CPT will encounter while carrying out its mission. While each operator trains for hundreds of potential situations, there are some nefarious individuals out there who have devised methods to counteract CP drills. Therefore, it is essential for CPTs to have the ability to be fluid and change according to the operational environment. For example, should the security of a building where a meeting is being held, or where the principal is staying, be compromised, the group may have to move quickly to exit and find an alternative venue, or move to a safe house to await further instructions.

RTAs take into consideration the mode of transport the principal is using: whether he/she is on foot or in a vehicle. Each scenario would have a different RTA, as each would require different skill sets. For example, ARW drivers have been trained in advanced driving techniques, giving them an excellent understanding of the performance of their vehicles and how to operate them under stressful conditions. Operative drivers can conduct evasive and offensive driving tactics at speed, as well as protection skills inside and outside the vehicle. They also have the ability to perform controlled and effective escape techniques while being pursued.

On the other hand, with the principal on foot, the CPT is presented with more areas to cover. Wide-open expanses, as well as narrow streets, offer a number of potential threats. Regardless of these areas of operations, the principal must be kept safe and secure at all times.

It is worth repeating: CP work is challenging, requiring

long hours and travel abroad. New locations require new SOPs to be implemented. Buildings, as well as other areas of operations, must be scouted in advance, noting avenues of entry and egress, as well vantage points that may be used for observation by a marksman or those directing an attack. Operatives must be flexible, require a high level of attention to detail and be able to communicate with all levels of management. They must also be able to adapt and change a plan without hesitation.

In recent years, the ARW was tasked with providing protection for some high-profile state visitors, such as Queen Elizabeth II when she came to Ireland in May 2011. Viable threats by dissident republicans saw the deployment of ARW airborne sniper teams in three Agusta-Westland AW139 helicopters. Counter-assault teams secured the motorcade and a number of ARW CP officers took up position alongside the queen and her entourage. Later that same month, United States President Barack Obama made a state visit to Ireland and received protection from the ARW. Both operations were a success.

In 2013 Ireland hosted the presidency of the Council of the European Union. This involved ARW sniper and spotter teams securing various areas and buildings used for the events. Also that year, the ARW was involved in security operations for the thirty-ninth G8 summit, which was held in Northern Ireland.

With the threat of attacks on prominent individuals increasing, the CP detail has become an important task for the ARW. It is essential that those operators entrusted with the mission are of the highest calibre, so as to ensure the protection and safety of those they are assigned to safeguard.

When the principal's day is finished, the CPT is still working, whether its members are carrying out recces, establishing a brief for the next day's operation, doing equipment checks or simply cleaning and refuelling the vehicles. No detail, however small, can be overlooked.

10

SOMALIA

The role of the ARW in overseas missions has increased dramatically over the years. Operatives from the unit have been deployed to Afghanistan, Iraq, Syria, Lebanon, Israel, Sudan, Ivory Coast, Liberia, Kosovo and Bosnia-Herzegovina as part of various international missions. One of the ARW's first overseas missions, as part of a UN force, was a deployment to Somalia in 1993.

Somalia, located in the Horn of Africa, has an estimated population of 14.3 million people. Bordered by Ethiopia to the west, Djibouti to the north-west, the Gulf of Aden to the north, the Indian Ocean to the east and Kenya to the south-west, Somalia has the longest coastline on Africa's mainland. Its terrain consists of plateaus, plains and highlands, and the country is noted for its climatically hot conditions that are prevalent all year round, with periodic monsoon winds and irregular rainfall. Once known as the Switzerland of Africa, Somalia was an affluent nation before it was decimated by civil war.

A former British and Italian colony, the country became

the Somali Democratic Republic when the Supreme Revolutionary Council seized power in 1969. In 1991 a number of Somali clans ousted President Siad Barre from power. Two clan leaders, Ali Mahdi and General Farah Aideed, orchestrated the rebellion, but they soon fell out. Civil war erupted between their two factions, leading to the deaths of 30,000 Somalis between 1991 and 1992. With the country in turmoil, famine spread throughout the region, resulting in the deaths of 200,000 people.

International aid agencies attempted to alleviate the effects of the famine but were unable to operate efficiently or provide humanitarian aid to urban or rural areas due to the looting of supply ships and aid convoys, the murder of aid workers and attacks on refugee centres. Roving bands of armed criminals and various factions continuously attacked aid convoys. Five or six gunmen would open fire on a convoy in the hope that it would stop. The food they looted would then be used as currency in a country whose population was on the brink of annihilation. Convoys and UN compounds were deemed soft targets by criminals and often came under attack. A Briton, Sean Devereux, and an Irish aid worker, Valerie Place, lost their lives in such attacks.

As a general rule, humanitarian convoys would not use armed escorts, but with the situation in Somalia rapidly deteriorating, armed escorts were soon deemed necessary as a 'last resort'. All other possibilities to reduce risks and ensure timely aid delivery had been exhaustively explored and determined to be unviable.

The initial UN mission and force sent to the country had proved inadequate and so, in November 1992, the UN charter was changed, with the mission becoming one of peace enforcement. Because of this change it was not covered by existing Irish law, and special legislation had to be enacted by the Irish government to allow this amendment to be included in the mandate of the Irish Defence Forces on UN service. 'Peace enforcement' is the use of military force in a conflict area, generally against the will of those combatants taking part in the conflict. In this case, a United States-led Unified Task Force (UNITAF) entered the conflict area and stabilised the situation, before handing over to the United Nations Operation in Somalia (UNOSOM) in May 1993.

The new UN mission had a revised mandate, which included the requirement to disarm the Somali factions. This was extremely dangerous. For example, on 5 June twenty-four Pakistani UNOSOM troops were killed in fighting with Aideed's organisation.

As part of the UNOSOM mission, an Irish Defence Forces contingent, consisting of the 1st and later the 2nd Transport Companies and the ARW, was deployed to Somalia in September 1993. It established an operating base known as Camp Shannon in the Baidoa region, 177 miles from the country's capital, Mogadishu. This secure military position would house the Irish troops along with over forty vehicles.

A number of ARW personnel were deployed on this mission. The operatives acclimatised to the heat and rugged conditions by working out of their base on a daily basis. One of the greatest tactical strengths of the ARW is its ability to mount operations in some of the world's harshest environments. Modern, high-tech equipment, together with the resilience and expert training of individual operatives, gives the Irish Defence Forces an elite unit that can fight anywhere, irrespective of the type of terrain or conditions encountered. Somalia was to test those deployed to their limits, with extremes of temperatures ranging from freezing cold at night to a stifling heat during the day.

As the situation within the country deteriorated, it became vital that food convoys got to their destinations unmolested. The Irish contingent was tasked with conducting what was to become known as the 'Mog Run', a supply run to Mogadishu. At the time, this was considered one of the most dangerous cities in the world. For example, it was there that American forces suffered heavy casualties in October 1993 when they launched a mission to capture leading figures in General Farah Aideed's clan in the centre of the city. In the Battle of Mogadishu, eighteen US soldiers, operating separately from UNOSOM, were killed.

From their base at Camp Shannon, the Irish peace-keepers would prepare for their weekly mission. The convoy consisted of about fifty personnel commanding over twenty vehicles, which included Man Diesel Trucks and Nissan Patrols. Initially, there was no armoured support and the unit knew that the soft-skinned vehicles would make easy targets. Heavy calibre machine guns were mounted on the front and rear vehicles in the convoy, and drivers knew not to stop if ambushed. The ARW was interspersed amongst the convoy, ready for action at any moment on the thirty-six hour operation.

Departing the base at 04.00 hours on a Monday morning, the group would travel along the route to Mogadishu, where it was joined by an escort provided by a contingent of UN troops from India. The convoy would arrive in the city by 10.00 hours, where loading of supplies and goods at the quays commenced. Early on Tuesday morning, they would set out to return to their base of operations at Camp Shannon with the supplies.

It was on one such return journey that the convoy was attacked. Sporadic gunfire directed at the vehicles from both sides of the road developed into an intense firefight, with the Irish and Indian troops successfully fighting off their attackers. Over ten insurgents were killed in the battle, while no Irish or Indian casualties were reported.

The Irish contingent was later equipped with two Patria Pasi (Sisu Pasi) armoured personnel carriers (APCs). These Finnish-manufactured, six-wheeled vehicles were given point and rear positions in the convoys, with the crew in both vehicles consisting of ARW personnel. If an attack was launched, these APCs could be manoeuvred to protect the rest of the vehicles in the group. With the ARW operatives on board, as well as the 12.7mm NSV machine guns mounted on the vehicles, the Irish contingent had continued success in their operations in the region.

Near to the Irish operations base, the Irish charity Goal had a compound. One night, an attack by enemy forces was launched on Goal's complex, with Irish Defence Forces personnel along with the ARW operatives coming to the charity's aid. As the troops arrived on the scene, they were engaged with small arms fire. A brief but intense firefight ensued, with the Irish contingent standing their ground. Ultimately, the attackers, realising they were up against professional soldiers and superior firepower, retreated back into the darkness. No casualties were reported for this action.

The ARW continued its mission in Somalia until September 1994, when the Irish contingent withdrew from the mission. Lieutenant Colonel Dorcha Lee, UNOSOM's senior officer (SO) co-ordinator, remained in his position until the mission came to a complete end in March 1995.

Sadly, peace and security still evades Somalia and its people.

EAST TIMOR

Around the turn of the millennium, many people in the Western world may have wondered where East Timor was; the ARW, however, was becoming very familiar with the territory. Its operatives were already on the ground, pathfinding for a new UN operation. Patrolling through an inhospitable jungle environment, as well as protecting the civilian population from Indonesian-backed militias, the Rangers proved themselves, once again, to be a capable special forces unit in the international arena.

Comprising the eastern half of the island of Timor, the nearby islands of Atauro and Jaco, and Oecusse, a small coastal enclave in the north-western half of the island, the country is 15,410 square kilometres (5,400 square miles) in size. It is surrounded on three sides by Indonesian West Timor, and separated from its southern neighbour, Australia, by the Timor Sea.

Since gaining independence from Portugal in 1974, East Timor had been under the control of Indonesia. The East Timorese are predominantly Roman Catholic, while the pro-Indonesian population of West Timor are Muslim. Since the 1970s there had been an atmosphere of religious, political and racial tension in the region. Then, on 30 August 1999, East Timor held a referendum in which it voted on whether to have greater autonomy or outright independence from Indonesia. When the province voted for independence, a wave of violence erupted.

Towns and villages were attacked by pro-Indonesian militias, which resulted in the deaths of many people and the destruction of much property. Burnt-out buildings, pockmarked by bullet holes, became a common feature of the region, many of them in the capital Dili. Ninety per cent of the town of Suai was damaged in a wave of attacks by militia forces. These guerrilla-style attacks were carried out throughout East Timor. The pro-Indonesian insurgency consisted of lightning attacks and small-scale actions, as well as economic sabotage. Morale amongst the general population plummeted as the number of casualties rose. The attackers, who knew the terrain, used the jungle to launch their attacks, as well as basing a refuge and supply depot with stores of ammunition and food there.

In response to the devastation and bloodshed, the UN established a multinational force in which Ireland would participate. The Australian-led operation also included troops from Thailand, Singapore, Malaysia, Canada, New Zealand, Italy, Denmark, Germany, Norway, France, the United States, Britain, the Republic of Korea, the Philippines and Portugal. This International Force East Timor (INTERFET) was established under UN Security Council Resolution 1264. Designated as a peacekeeping mission, the mandate was to restore peace and security to East Timor, to protect and support the UN Mission in East Timor (UNAMET) in carrying out their tasks, and to facilitate humanitarian assistance operations. In a nutshell, they were going to restore the peace.

In October 1999 operatives from the 1st Platoon ARW arrived in Darwin, Australia, where they commenced ten days of pre-deployment training with the Australian Army. This consisted of acclimatising, as well as briefings about the situation on the ground, the terrain and the hostiles that the Rangers might encounter. The unit was deployed to the town of Suai, which held the New Zealand battalion headquarters. For tactical communications (TACCOM) purposes, the men were assigned to the New Zealand recce company, with an ARW officer being installed as the Company 2 I/C, which allowed for effective SOF command and control.

The first three weeks of the deployment saw the ARW working out of their compound in Suai. Here they carried out extensive patrols, both on foot and in vehicles, securing and maintaining supply routes within the battalion's AO. This also involved facilitating humanitarian aid, guaranteeing the safety of locals and ensuring the safe return of displaced persons from West to East Timor. In addition, they detained several suspected militiamen, as well as conducting a 'hearts and minds' campaign with locals (a method used to bring a subjugated population on side). Their presence was a reassurance for many who had been living in fear.

There was a UN air component to the mission, consisting of fixed wing and rotary air support. The ARW was tasked with flying to remote village areas where they carried out threat assessments regarding possible militia activity. These were short missions and the intel gathered was relayed back to battalion HQ.

The ARW was ultimately deployed into the mountainous border area between East and West Timor to carry out deep-penetration jungle ops. Much of the country is mountainous; its highest point, the peak of Tatamailau – also known as Mount Ramelau – is 2,963 metres (9,721 feet) above sea level. The climate is tropical and generally dry and humid, and is characterised by distinct dry and rainy seasons.

The unit established an OP in an abandoned building just outside the village of Taroman. This was used as a jungle operations base and could be resupplied easily. The unit's AO consisted of a 10-kilometre stretch of border, six villages and the surrounding dwellings and farmlands.

Working from their OP, the Rangers had a tactical benefit in controlling and monitoring the only road/track suitable for vehicles entering the region.

Border incursions by armed militias had destabilised the region and so the Rangers were tasked with securing the AO. By operating in small numbers, they moved quickly and quietly though the jungle. The hope was that by succeeding in dominating the AO, it would make the region safe for local inhabitants to return. In order to achieve this, the unit had to control the terrain through continuous long-range patrolling.

Conventional thinking is that operating in a jungle environment can only be done for a few days because of the harsh environment. However, the ARW deployed small patrols for long periods. They also established 'stop gaps' at known militia crossing points from West to East Timor, so as to hinder the militia's previously safe passage.

The terrain was difficult, often impenetrable. The soldiers found the jungle environment hot and humid, dank and wet, full of venomous insects and snakes, and difficult to navigate. However, the ARW soon mastered the cornerstones of jungle warfare. The key is to get close to the enemy forces before they realise you are there and, with the Rangers' skill in both concealment and stealth, they were able to patrol undetected. The soldiers waded through leech-infested waters, swatted countless mosquitoes and hacked their way through miles of impenetrable, wet jungle foliage. Working in this environment also heightened their operational skills, as their senses of smell, sight, sound and taste adapted to their surroundings. The crack of a twig, the sight of a damaged flower, the smell and taste of the air notified a patrol that the enemy was or had been in the vicinity.

The Irish soldiers also befriended the remaining locals who hadn't fled the conflict, reassuring them with their presence. This 'hearts and minds' technique worked and led to locals often reporting sightings of enemy incursions in the area. These extra eyes and ears were a great resource and enabled the ARW to check any incursions and neutralise any threat. Some militia personnel attempted to return to their villages, but the locals informed on them to the ARW, who then apprehended them and handed them over to the authorities. Acting on intelligence from the Australian and New Zealand (J2) cells, the ARW also conducted a number of operations that involved raiding villages to extract persons of interest. Often operating at night, ARW teams were deployed by helicopter or trudged through miles of jungle to get to their quarry.

Within a few months, the ARW, through dominating the terrain, had stabilised the region, securing the area and providing a safe haven for the inhabitants. Their presence reassured the population that the international community did care and would, for the foreseeable future, continue to defend, protect and support.

In February 2000 INTERFET handed over command of military operations to the United Nations Transitional Administration in East Timor (UNTAET). The second ARW unit deployed in the region completed its four-month deployment in June 2000, with subsequent rotations being carried out by regular infantry platoons. The mission came to an end in May 2004.

12

LIBERIA

While the operation in East Timor may have been one of the ARW's toughest assignments, Liberia was to be one of its deadliest.

The United Nations Mission in Liberia (UNMIL) was established under the United Nations Security Council Resolution 1509 on 1 October 2003. The decision to deploy the ARW to Liberia came on foot of a specific request from the director of peacekeeping operations in UN headquarters, New York, for a unit that would, under the direct command of UNMIL's force commander, carry out 'special operation' missions.

While serving with UNMIL, the ARW was renamed the 'Special Operations Task Group' (SOTG). The force commander, Lieutenant General Daniel Opande, was briefed on what the ARW could provide. The Rangers were then tasked with supplying special reconnaissance, human intelligence, liaison, and hostage rescue or extraction mission capabilities. The ARW's AO was all of Liberia, a country of considerable size and dangers.

The Republic of Liberia is located on the west coast of Africa. Covering an area of 111,369 square kilometres (43,000 square miles), the country is bordered by Sierra Leone to its north-west, Guinea to the north and Côte d'Ivoire to the east. The Atlantic Ocean sweeps against the coast of the country. The population is estimated to be in the region of 4,700,000 people. The climate is equatorial, with significant rainfall between May and October. Forests on the coastline consist of salt-tolerant mangrove trees, while the more sparsely populated inland area has plateaus of drier grasslands.

In 1989 civil war erupted in Liberia and continued until 1997, resulting in the deaths of an estimated 150,000 people. Law and order collapsed and the deteriorating situation in the country threatened to spill over into Sierra Leone, Guinea and Côte d'Ivoire. International intervention did little to alleviate the violence. In 1997 Charles Taylor of the National Patriotic Party was elected president. However, his followers, known as the Government of Liberia (GOL) forces, continued human rights abuses, including the exclusion and harassment of political opponents and the failure to reform the security services. These acts, as well as ongoing differences between opposing groups, contributed to a resumption of conflict in the country.

Taylor's regime was under threat from the Liberians

United for Reconciliation and Democracy (LURD), who were based in the north-western Lofa region. A major offensive was launched against Taylor's forces in 2001 by LURD, and by 2002 they had advanced to within 50 kilometres of the capital, Monrovia. By 2003 they were through to the coast and just 20 kilometres from the capital. To add to Taylor's woes, another group, the Movement for Democracy in Liberia (MODEL) had launched an offensive in the south of the country. By July 2003 LURD had captured three of Monrovia's ports, with MODEL seizing the remaining port.

In response to the impending humanitarian crisis in Liberia, in August the UN Security Council passed Resolution 1497, authorising the intervention of a multi-national peacekeeping force from the Economic Community of West African States (ECOWAS), pending the deployment of a UN stabilisation force.

While the peacekeepers had to deal with three heavily armed factions, they also had to contend with armed militias and gangsters who were exploiting the political situation for personal gain. Armed with an assortment of weapons, and driving technicals (a light improvised fighting vehicle, typically open-backed), these groups plundered at will and terrorised innocent people.

In November 2003 the Irish Defence Forces, as part of the UN mission, deployed to the region. The ARW had located and secured a base to work from that was situated in the grounds of an abandoned hotel, 10 kilometres north of Monrovia. It was designated Camp Clara. The unit was initially tasked with securing its immediate AO, as well as conducting security on UN convoys. It was while providing convoy support that the ARW would suffer a fatality.

Two weeks into the operation, on 27 November 2003, operating 40 kilometres south of Monrovia, a UN convoy consisting of nine vehicles, with ARW support, was conducting a routine patrol. The roads were treacherous, with bad surfacing. Some were little more than tracks. Along with the bad conditions, the convoys were under constant threat of ambush. Midway through this patrol, the lead vehicle, a Land Rover 110, swerved sharply as it negotiated a left-hand bend. The vehicle left the road and tumbled down a steep embankment, rolling three times before coming to a standstill.

Medics were quickly on the scene and the three soldiers inside were extracted from the vehicle and medevaced to the Dutch medical ship *Rotterdam*. Sadly, Sergeant Derec Mooney died from his injuries. Of the other two Rangers, one was treated for serious injuries, while the other was able to return to Camp Clara.

Though this tragic event affected the unit, the Rangers knew that it was imperative that they continue with the mission, as the main Irish contingent was en route to the country.

The 90th Infantry Battalion soon arrived, consisting of a logistical/administration company, an APC company, and a support company consisting of 450 personnel. Taken from the 4th Western Brigade, the Irish soldiers took on the task of providing UNMIL's QRF. This consisted of an APC company with twenty-two Mowag APCs. These were supported by the logistical and administration companies, and support companies, which comprised medical platoons, military police, ordnance sections and a national support element. The support company also included an engineer platoon, an 81mm mortar platoon and a cavalry troop equipped with AML 20s and AML 90s (panard-type vehicles). The QRF's mission was one of long-range 'recce in force' patrols, as well as providing rapid reaction to any emergency that may arise in any of UNMIL's four military sectors.

The SOTG conducted long-range patrols, many in excess of nine days' duration, in the remote areas of Liberia that were either outside UNMIL control or where there were reports of activity by former combatants. The SOTG operations included insertions by land, sea and air, the latter being made by Ukrainian Mi-26s, which were capable of transporting the unit's specially adapted reconnaissance vehicles.

Although providing humanitarian assistance was not a direct task of the SOTG, it became a regular feature in the form of medical assistance provided to the local population by the unit's medical officer (MO) and patrol medics. This 'hearts and minds' campaign enabled the SOTG to gain vital intelligence from the locals in relation to the whereabouts and actions of local militia groups.

On 6 January 2004, acting on intelligence received, an SOTG unit was dispatched to rescue a group of civilians being held against their will by renegade GOL forces. An estimated thirty civilians were being held captive in a 40-foot container near the town of Yekepa. Twenty armed Rangers were flown out in a Ukranian Mi-26 helicopter at 12.00 hours, arriving soon after in Gbapa in the northern sector of Nimba County, close to the border with Guinea. Moving rapidly to the village, the Rangers took the enemy by surprise, securing the release of what turned out to be thirty-five captives that included men, women and children. Faced with specialist forces, many militia members fled into the bush, while the Rangers succeeded in capturing the commander and deputy commander of the renegade force. They were taken to a nearby police station that had been secured by the patrol. Many of the people rescued were brought to a local medical facility, where they received treatment for beatings and rapes inflicted upon them while in captivity.

The ARW was involved in other similar operations while deployed in Liberia, rescuing people and disarming aggressors from numerous factions. The Rangers' actions in Liberia drew praise from the international community and boosted the reputation of the Irish special forces worldwide.

13

CHAD

In 2008 the ARW was deployed, along with other European special forces units, as 'Initial Entry Forces' to Chad and the Central African Republic (CAR) as part of a UN-mandated, EU-led peacekeeping operation. This EU mission was mandated under UN Security Council Resolution 1778, to operate in Eastern Chad and work in conjunction with the civilian UN mission in the region, which was known as United Nations Mission in the Central African Republic and Chad (MINURCAT).

The fifth largest country in Africa, Chad is landlocked, being bordered by Libya to the north, Sudan to the east, the CAR to the south and Cameroon, Niger and Nigeria to the west. Years of political instability and civil war ravaged the country, leading to a humanitarian crisis. In 2008 a United Nations report on Chad highlighted the deteriorating situation and the presence of thousands of refugees from the Sudan's Darfur region and others from the CAR, as well as 170,000 'Internally Displaced Persons'.

The operational headquarters for the UN mission was

based in Paris, France, and was conducted by Lieutenant General Pat Nash of the Irish Defence Forces. He was in command of a force of 3,700 troops from numerous EU countries that included Austria, Sweden, France and Belgium. Known as EUFOR Chad/CAR, its mission was to protect the increasing number of refugees and internally displaced persons in Eastern Chad. The ultimate goal of the mission was to bring stability to the region that would, in time, allow people to return to their homes, mostly in Darfur. The force was to remain impartial in the conflict itself.

Fifty-eight Rangers were sent ahead of the main contingent, as well as HQ staff. On 24 April 2008 the 147-man advance party arrived in Chad to commence the construction of Camp Ciara. Located in Goz Beida in south-eastern Chad, it would be from here that the Rangers and the Irish battalion would commence operations.

Having secured the surrounding areas with assistance from other EU special forces units, the ARW was tasked with demonstrating a robust presence in the AO. Using special forces overtly instead of covertly shows the opposition that a specialist unit is in that country to protect the vulnerable and displaced, and that force, if necessary, is an option.

The ARW reverted to smaller teams and made ready to conduct long-range reconnaissance patrols. This key military task consists of heavily armed reconnaissance teams patrolling deep into hostile territory for days or weeks on end. Specialist equipment and transport are vital for carrying out these types of operations.

Vehicles and weapons are a key element in the capabilities of the ARW. Reliable, powerful and accurate, they must be up to the operational task in hand. With the continuously deteriorating state of affairs in Chad, the ARW had a veritable arsenal of weapons at its disposal, as well as robust vehicles, to deal with any situation that arose. Operatives carried individual weapons such as the Heckler & Koch assault rifle and machine guns, as well as the Steyr AUG A3, a variant of the weapon that was on general issue to the Irish Defence Forces, which was capable of being fitted with a M203 grenade launcher. Heavy support weapons consisted of AT4 SRAAW short range anti-armour weapons and grenade launchers. Squad support weapons were FN 7.62mm general purpose machine guns (GPMGs) with a rate of fire of 750 rounds per minute.

For conducting the long-range reconnaissance patrols, units were equipped with Ford F350 special reconnaissance vehicles (SRVs). These SRVs were armed with Browning M2 .50-calibre heavy machine guns (HMGs), as well as GPMGs, and were capable of driving through some of the world's worst terrain.

Upon stocking up with munitions, fuel and rations to last a number of weeks in the field, units moved out from their base towards their AOs. Groups conducted route reconnaissance, familiarising themselves with their AO, collating and relaying information back to HQ on the conditions and safety of roads and whether they were suitable and secure for aid convoys to use. They identified sites for possible air strips and forward operating bases (FOBs) throughout the region. They liaised with village elders and the local populace, gleaning information on the strengths and deployments of militias, rebels and bandits. They identified safe havens, as well as noting areas that could prove unsafe for humanitarian aid workers.

The ARW was permitted to engage hostile forces if necessary under the UN terms for the EUFOR mission to Chad and the CAR. This covered responses to attacks or criminal acts on refugees, aid groups, Irish or other EUFOR personnel and internally displaced persons. However, contrary to popular belief, special force units conducting long-range reconnaissance patrols do not engage with the enemy unless absolutely necessary.

One Ranger patrol, consisting of a number of vehicles and thirty operatives, was tasked with patrolling eastwards along the border with Darfur in Sudan. Those travelling on the patrol knew that any border has the potential for trouble and the Rangers knew that 'contact' was a possibility. This particular AO had been classified by EUFOR as a zone of maximum danger, or 'Red Zone'. The patrol came upon the isolated village of Ade in the vicinity of Modoya. Deciding to investigate, part of the patrol was sent in to recce the village. The remaining Rangers set up positions covering the approaches to the village, as well as providing 'overwatch' for those who went into the hamlet.

It was then that an estimated 200 armed rebels emerged from the village, confronting the Irish soldiers who had entered. These rebels had participated in an attack on N'Djamena weeks previously, almost succeeding in capturing the capital. With one element of the ARW patrol in the village and the others on the outskirts, the situation was in danger of escalating. Both sides were taken by surprise by the presence of the other. A tense stand-off ensued, with both sides holding their ground and, more importantly, their fire. Dialogue was opened up between the two groups through the patrol's interpreter. This was the first time that EUFOR troops had established contact with one of the rebel groups. Realising that the Irish were not Chadian government forces and were impartial in the military and political situation in the country, the rebels relaxed their stance. The two groups continued talking before each pulled back.

The Rangers returned to their base of operations, reporting the meeting with the rebel group. Tact, not force, had saved the unit from a potentially deadly situation, as well as allowing them to gather important intelligence. With this information, vital tactical and strategic decisions were made that enabled the main contingent of EUFOR to operate freely and safely throughout the region.

In the months that followed, the mission in Chad continued, with hundreds of Irish troops serving in the country, rotating every four months. Following a decision by the Chadian president, Idriss Deby, to withdraw support for the MINURCAT military mission, the Irish battalion withdrew in April 2010. Irish staff officers remained until the mission finally closed on 28 December 2010.

14

MALI

In September 2019 the ARW was deployed to the West African country of Mali as part of the UN Multi-dimensional Integrated Stabilization Mission in Mali (MINUSMA), which was established in April 2013 after an upsurge in violence in the region. The mission has been described by the UN and military officials as the most dangerous UN peacekeeping mission in the world.

Mali, a former French colony, is a landlocked nation in West Africa. At 1,242,248 square kilometres (480,000 square miles), it is the world's twenty-fourth largest country. Consisting of eight regions, it is comparable in size to South Africa. The country's borders on the north reach deep into the inhospitable Sahara desert, while the mountainous terrain of the Adrar des Ifoghas massif lies in the north-east. The south of the country, where the majority of its inhabitants reside, features the Niger and Senegal rivers.

In January 2012 a Tuareg rebellion – an uprising against the Malian government that hoped to attain independence for the northern region of the country – began in northern

Mali, leading to a period of instability in the region. This volatility provided an opportunity for extremist Islamic groups, including Ansar Dine and Al-Qaeda, to turn on the Tuaregs and exploit the chaotic situation, advancing south at speed and seizing control of key objectives – communications networks, military posts, etc. – with the aim of implementing Sharia law in Mali. According to the UN, it is estimated that thousands of people fled south in order to avoid the fighting.

Western powers became increasingly concerned that Mali might be used as a staging area for terrorist attacks throughout the world. On 11 January 2013 French Armed Forces, at the behest of the Malian government, intervened and began military operations in Mali. This operation, known as Operation Serval, was the beginning of military intervention in the country, carried out in order to restore law and order and support the Malian government. French forces deployed 2,500 troops to bolster the Malian Army and, using the country's capital, Bamako, as a FOB, they went on the offensive. After a number of battles, French and Malian forces retook a number of strategically located towns, forcing the insurgents to fall back along the Algerian border. There, the insurgents resorted to guerrilla tactics against government forces. There are currently an estimated 4,000 French troops still on active service within Mali.

An EU training mission was implemented in February

2013 to provide the Malian armed forces with military training and advice in order to improve their capacity to maintain security in Mali and restore the authority of the Malian government and territorial integrity of the Malian state. The Irish Defence Forces deployed a number of personnel on this mission, offering training in bomb disposal and clearing landmines.

The UN Security Council deployed peacekeepers in April 2013, who became the targets of a fierce insurgent campaign. A 2015 peace deal signed by Mali's government and separatist groups failed to end the violence. Since then the situation has deteriorated, as attacks by Islamic extremists against civilians have escalated and intercommunal violence has killed hundreds and precipitated a humanitarian crisis.

Islamist armed groups affiliated to Al-Qaeda have increased attacks in the region, targeting Malian security forces, UN peacekeepers and international forces in northern and central Mali. Many civilians have been killed, primarily by the indiscriminate use of IEDs planted along major roads. Furthermore, armed insurgents continue to threaten and kill villagers who are deemed to have collaborated with the authorities. They also impose their version of Sharia law via courts that do not adhere to a fair trial.

During 2018 at least 300 civilians were killed in

over 100 incidents of communal violence in central and northern Mali. The violence pitted ethnically aligned self-defence groups against communities accused of supporting Islamist-armed groups, resulting in the pillage and destruction of dozens of villages and the displacement of thousands of people. In June 2019 100 villagers were killed in an overnight attack on a village in central Mali.

In addition to the UN force, there is also a separate anti-insurgency operation being conducted, which was established by the G5 Sahel leaders. This is an institutional framework for the coordination of regional cooperation in development policies and security matters in West Africa. The Sahel group consists of Burkina Faso, Chad, Mali, Mauritania and Niger. This cross-border joint force is intended to fight terrorism, eliminate organised cross-border criminal gangs, and put an end to human trafficking in the region. The UN force provides operational and logistical support, while the larger French military contingent is deployed as part of Operation Barkhane (an ongoing anti-insurgent operation in Africa's Sahel region) and works alongside the separate G5 Sahel joint-terrorism force.

The ARW deployment to Mali comprises fourteen operatives in total, with a mix of four- and six-month deployments over a twenty-four month period. Working as a team, they have been tasked with contributing to the ongoing security and stability of a country that many see as a potential threat to security in the entire region and beyond. They will form part of a larger German-led intelligence, surveillance and reconnaissance company, as well as aiding with intelligence-gathering operations. This is the Rangers' first major deployment since Chad. They are not operating in isolation and will have the benefit of the protection and medical support that's in place for the larger company.

Though the military in Mali have access to drones, spy planes and advanced SIGINT from orbiting satellites, as well as electronic technology for mapping out enemy forces and terrain, gathering intelligence via patrolling remains a very important aspect of the ARW's role. After all, there is only so much that a satellite can relay to command and control. To really understand the enemy, ears and eyes on the ground are essential.

In Timbuktu, there has been an increase in intercommunal violence. Investigating these incidents and tracking those who are orchestrating these violent acts will just be one part of the ARW's mission. Working on the ground, the operatives will face the threat of firefights, ambushes and roadside IEDs in remote and hostile environments. As of September 2019, more than 201 people deployed by the UN have been killed there since the outbreak of hostilities.

The ARW's service as part of this mission in one of the world's poorest and most fragile regions will lend support to some of the world's most vulnerable people.

This mission is currently ongoing.

The decision by the Irish government to send the ARW to Mali, as well as other conflict zones throughout the world, was, according to government sources, 'taken after careful planning and consideration and demonstrates Ireland's commitment to UN peace and security'.

WHAT WE DO IN THE SHADOWS

15

MAKING THE CUT TODAY
SPECIAL OPERATIONS FORCE QUALIFICATION

While the course has changed somewhat since the 1980s, the high standards expected by the ARW have not. The ARW has significantly revised its selection and assessment procedures for prospective unit members in recent years. The selection and basic skills courses have been replaced by a new single course combining the two, which is now called the Special Operations Force Qualification (SOFQ).

While this course may seem daunting to many, there is help on hand for potential candidates. The ARW strength and conditioning coach has devised what is known as the Sustainable Function Programme (SFP), which is designed to help ARW candidates prepare properly for the demands of the SOFQ process in the four months before the course commences. The SFP emphasises physical preparation for SOFQ MOD 1 – Assessment & Selection. (SOFQ MOD 1 is designed to select candidates who have the potential for further training in the SOFQ process.)

As with many special forces qualification courses, SOFQ is both physically and mentally demanding, with a high attrition rate. However, with the correct preparation any motivated soldier, sailor or airman can pass SOFQ MOD 1 and put themselves in the position to continue through the SOFQ modules. Candidates are expected to be injury free and possess a high level of fitness, as this is an extended strenuous period of PT.

The reason for this high level is that every operational member of the ARW is unique, as each is trained to perform a task that is vital to the successful completion of the mission. The physical demands placed on an opera-tive and the unpredictable nature of service in the ARW require that unit members maintain an excellent standard of physical fitness, be adaptable and be ready to face the challenges that they will encounter head on. Physical fit-ness is seen as a critical attribute for an ARW operator. Therefore, the physical demands placed on ARW candi-dates during the SOFQ process reflect the actual job demands.

The SFP is fifteen weeks in total. It is recommended that candidates achieve a minimum Grade 4 on the Defence Forces' annual fitness assessment before commencing this syllabus. (Grades go from 1 to 6, 1 being elite fitness.)

The course consists of four distinct stages:

Stage 1 (Weeks 1–6): This is the initial preparation phase to prepare the body and mind for Stage 2. Stage 1 concentrates on improving the candidate's mobility, core strength and general conditioning. The training sessions are structured to ensure maximum recovery and that the candidate adapts physically as the exercises progress. Completion of Stage 1 is essential for the less-fit candidate. This helps mitigate the risk of injury moving forward. Those candidates who are of a higher level of fitness are allowed to progress to Week 4 of the SFP after completing the fitness check.

Stage 2 (Weeks 7–12): This is the core stage of the SFP. It is here that the hard work takes place and physical and mental robustness is developed in advance of SOFQ MOD 1. Stage 2 incorporates two three-week phases. Both phases culminate with a demanding training week. The type of training varies during this training week, but tends to consistently include long hours, many of which are spent, day and night, in rough terrain and inclement weather. Training days within this week also involve two training sessions and two hill days, spent trekking through difficult terrain while being timed. Completion of Stage 2 is essential to progress.

Stage 3 (Week 13): This is the most demanding week

in the training with three hill days. This stage should be undertaken with caution. Elements of this training week can either be removed or reduced in duration and intensity if the candidate feels that injury is likely. However, this week helps the candidate develop their resilience and confidence in anticipation for SOFQ MOD 1.

Stage 4 (Week 14–15): This is the culmination of the SFP. In this stage, the candidate completes a fitness check and a prolonged taper (i.e. test). This taper is essential to ensure that the candidate is in optimal physical condition for commencing SOFQ MOD 1. The aim of all those competing is to peak on the 'Endurance', which is the culminating test of the SFP. It involves a 60-kilometre hike over mountainous terrain carrying 60 pounds +, while averaging 4 kilometres per hour.

Having completed the SFP course, candidates attend the SOFQ preparation and orientation course. This course is conducted annually in May or June. It is one week in duration and gives the SOFQ candidate an excellent insight into the SOFQ process and operational service in the ARW. The week's training concentrates on developing the candidate's ability to navigate in mountain terrain during both day and night, and in all weather conditions. There is an emphasis on the candidate's physical and mental preparation in advance of SOFQ. This tuition is provided by ARW task unit members and ARW strength and conditioning coaches in co-operation with Defence Forces physiotherapists. The SFP and process involved in preparing for SOFQ MOD 1 is very demanding and so it is recommended that soldiers discuss with their unit commanders the demands of the course and the time required in preparing for selection before committing to the course. It is also important to keep in mind that during this period, and while on SOFQ, it will be difficult to maintain a work–life balance.

If several candidates from the same unit intend to participate in SOFQ MOD 1, then group training is strongly recommended. There are a number of training aids available for candidates, which are available to soldiers through their unit's physical training instructor (PTI). Defence Forces physiotherapists have been working closely with the ARW in an effort to understand, measure, adapt to and inform elements of training to ensure optimal performance and injury prevention. From their examination of the course, these physiotherapists stress the need for candidates to prepare adequately for the level of strenuous physical activity involved. The SFP offers an excellent and measured approach to building resilience for undertaking the SOFQ course.

Having undertaken the preliminary courses recommended for SOFQ selection, soldiers will find themselves standing on the square at Plunkett Barracks. The course is open to all ranks of the Irish Defence Forces who possess high levels of physical fitness, navigation skills, personal motivation and the aspiration to serve in the ARW. The SOFQ syllabus is designed to test and assess all aspects of the candidate's character, military skills, ability and general suitability for becoming a member of the ARW. It also provides the potential unit member with all the skills and knowledge necessary to function in the role of SOF assault team operator on successful completion of the course.

The SOFQ course is thirty-eight weeks long and is divided into five distinct modules:

Module 1: Assessment and Evaluation

Module 2: Skills and Leadership

Module 3: SOF Tactics, Techniques and Procedures (TTPs)

Module 4: Counter-terrorism TTPs

Module 5: Continuation Training

The objective of Module 1 is to assess the candidate's levels of physical fitness, motivation and suitability to progress onwards to SOFQ Modules 2–5. During Phase 1 of this module, all candidates must pass a series of fitness assessments, map reading and individual navigation assessments, as well as claustrophobia, water confidence and psychometric testing in order to progress to Phase 2. The candidate is then assessed further by a series of individual navigation exercises with set weights but unknown distances and completion times, culminating in a 60-kilometre cross-country march while carrying a 65-pound combat load. Officer candidates are also subjected to rigorous assessment of their planning and decision-making skills to assess their suitability to achieve a command appointment within the ARW.

The pass rate for Module 1 in the last number of years has been approximately twenty per cent. While injury is always a factor in the SOFQ process, voluntary withdrawal was the primary reason why candidates did not progress to Module 2, followed closely by test failure. In order to be successful, candidates must stay true to their reasons for being on SOFQ. It is tough, but remember, it is simply a means to an end: becoming an ARW SOF operator.

At the commencement of Module 2, SOFQ candidates who are of private rank are then promoted to the rank of Acting Corporal and are in receipt of ARW allowances. Modules 2–5 consist of further training and assessment in areas such as SOF weapons and marksmanship, live fire tactical training (LFTT), SOF conventional and CT TTPs, combat water survival, survival evasion resistance extraction (SERE), and communications and medical training. Candidates are awarded the 'Fianóglach' tab on successful completion of Module 3; they are assigned to the unit and awarded the distinctive ARW green beret on completion of Module 4. Candidates are also promoted to the rank of substantive corporal on conclusion of this module. During Module 5, SOFQ candidates receive further training in military leadership, as well as SRV weapons training.

On conclusion of the SOFQ course, candidates are posted to an operational ARW task unit as an assault team operator. They can expect to undertake further training in areas such as advanced medical skills, military free fall, combat diving and boat handling, close protection, and advanced weapons skills. The overall pass rate for the SOFQ course (Modules 1–5) is fifteen per cent. Of those candidates that pass, forty per cent are on their second (or more) attempt. There is no doubt that the SOFQ course is inherently tough. It is designed to test character, military skills and physical fitness over an extended period. What it takes to succeed is proper mental and physical preparation, coupled with personal motivation and a desire to serve in the ARW.

16

IN THE CROSS HAIRS

Special forces throughout the world employ snipers in three main roles: in the field (conventional or counter-insurgency warfare), in the urban environment, or for specific ARW missions. The most important and vital role of a sniper, operating either alone or with a partner, is to pin down or disrupt a large enemy force by killing senior officers or by disrupting its communications, thereby denying the enemy its command and control capability in the space of two or three seconds.

Since the foundation of the ARW in 1980, sniping has become one of the core specialist skills employed by the unit, with candidates being tested on marksmanship principals and shooting on the range. In 1985 this was formalised into the first 'Sniper Instructors' Course', conducted by Regimental Sergeant Major Frank Faughnan and Sergeant Vinnie Carroll. A second course was conducted in 1986.

The primary qualities considered when selecting a man for sniper training are good eyesight and ice-cool nerves.

However, marksmanship ability in itself is not enough. A high level of camouflage and concealment skills, as well as advanced fieldcraft, are other essential skills needed for the sniper to be effective in the field. For example, they must be able to move across open terrain without being spotted by the enemy, and select concealed firing positions that offer a good field of fire, as well as an avenue of egress once the target or targets have been engaged.

The first sniper course conducted by the ARW lasted five weeks and consisted of instruction in sight and wind adjustment, range practices, navigation, training, and camouflage and concealment. Students took part in shoots at the Kilcoran range using the FN rifle. Sniper rifles are specialist weapons and are designed to meet specific operational standards in the hands of a skilled operative. They are considered one of the most deadly and selective weapons on the field of battle. While the shooter is trained to a high standard, the rifle also must meet a standard.

In the late 1980s ARW snipers experimented with the HK PSG1 semi-automatic sniper rifle with its own dedicated optical sight. The weapon proved suitable for counter-terrorism operations, but it was felt that a more powerful weapon was required for conventional training and field operations.

By liaising with other specialist forces throughout the

world, the ARW was able to maintain and expand its understanding of the necessary skills of sniping, as well as getting a better sense of the best weapons to use within the unit. In 1990 the ARW purchased the Accuracy International PM .308 sniper rifle with its Schmidt and Bender 6x42 sight. Two years later, in 1992, the Irish Defence Forces purchased more Accuracy sniper rifles, which promoted an upsurge in interest in the skills of sniping.

After personnel from the Infantry Weapons Wing (IWW) attended a sniper course in the UK in the early 1990s, Captain Michael Broderick and Sergeant Seán Cahill conducted an ARW basic and instructors sniper course with a new syllabus that augmented previous courses. Upon completion of this revised course, students – after passing a range of subjects – were then able to qualify as a sniper/instructor. The subjects included shooting, stalking, observation, camouflage and concealment, map reading, judging distance and sniper knowledge.

All ARW operatives are taught how to maintain their weapons, but for a trained sniper the standards are far higher. Too much oil in the rifle, for example, will create a telltale smoke 'signature' that will reveal the sniper's position. A shiny barrel or other part of the weapon may reflect sunlight, once again endangering the operative. Sniper rifles are also generally less robust than other military guns, especially their optics, which have to be treated with great care. The correct calibre and type of ammunition for the weapon and mission are as important as the skills required to use them.

By late 1993, as a result of the developments in the unit's training and operational experience, the ARW established a dedicated sniper team named Sierra Team. A sniper team consists of a sniper and spotter. The two-man team or 'buddy system' offers many advantages over the deployment of a lone sniper in the field. The spotter carries his own scope, which is much more powerful than the scope on the rifle. The spotter uses his scope to help the sniper observe objectives and set up the shot. It is vital that the two soldiers work together in getting to the objective undetected, setting up their position, waiting for the target and taking the shot. Once the shot is taken, the spotter watches it to help the sniper readjust his aim or position in the unlikely event that he misses his target. The high-velocity, long-range rounds used in sniper rifles leave a vapour trail as they fly through the air. The spotter can track a shot by watching for this vapour trail. The spotter also has the important task of protecting the shooter. For this, an ARW spotter will carry a HK417 assault rifle. Sniper teams often work behind enemy lines and depend on each other for survival.

These soldiers can also function as a lead response and

recce element (i.e. reconnaissance unit) who are able to respond to operational situations rapidly. Close target recce (CTR) (i.e. tracking the enemy's movements through various means) is a vital element of ARW operations, with snipers often leading the way in this sort of mission. Some operatives even undergo the 'Recce Commander's Course' to augment their skills in this discipline.

Sierra Team is now the focus for sniper training within the ARW. A large percentage of the current training programme focuses on precise and accurate shooting in the different environments in which a sniper may be required to operate. A sniper's involvement in a conventional deployment, for example, usually revolves around accuracy from a great distance, whereas in a counter-terrorism situation, the sniper's role often requires greater accuracy at shorter ranges, sometimes encompassing non-lethal shooting.

Working with its European counterparts, the ARW has conducted co-ordinated shoots, testing weapons and calibres, as well as shooting through objects. In 1997 the ARW sniper cadre, led by Captain John Whittaker and Sergeants Seán Cahill and Sean B., conducted an urban sniper course that was attended by other European special forces operatives. The attendees were instructed in all aspects of a sniper's work in an urban environment. For many urban missions it is the sniper's job to provide 'over-watch' of the operations area. Basically, this means that from his position he must carefully study every threat and, if necessary, identify the ones to eliminate in order to clear a path and protect the team on the ground. This difficult task requires the operative to use maximum diligence, as they will have friendlies and civilians in close proximity, as well as the enemy.

ARW operatives attend sniping courses overseas, as well as taking part in international shooting competitions. The unit excels at these competitions, having come first on many occasions and in numerous categories.

Today the ARW possess the .338 Accuracy International rifle and the 7.62 Accuracy International model AW. The weapons are mounted with Accuracy Schmidt and Bender MIL MKII 5-25x56 sights. These weapons and sights guarantee greater accuracy at longer ranges and allow for greater planning ranges.

The AW50-F12.7mm rifle is used in an anti-materiel role. This type of weapon is designed for use against military equipment (materiel) rather than against other combatants (anti-personnel). Spotters carry the HK417-7.62mm spotting scope. Night vision equipment and wind meters to aid the team in their wind estimation are also carried.

While advances in technology, weapons and training have made today's sniper a valuable asset on the battlefield, it is the soldier behind the weapon, looking through the cross hairs, which makes an ARW sniper such a deadly force multiplier.

17

BY NEPTUNE'S BEARD

Living on the island of Ireland means that being able to perform covert infiltration and extraction by seaborne methods is a high priority for the ARW. Trained in sub-aqua and surface swimming skills, and the techniques required to use small craft, the unit has the capability to hit hard and fast from the sea.

Naval or marine specialist units have responsibility for a variety of missions related to their ability to operate on, under or near the water. These include: maritime counter-terrorism, protection of assets such as ships or oil platforms, aid to the civil power in drug suppression or other smuggling operations, beach reconnaissance, hydro-graphical surveying, recovery of sensitive or classified equipment from under the water, rescue of downed airmen in the sea, reconnaissance of enemy installations near the coast, raids along the coastline, and maritime and riverine counter-insurgency.

With these aspects in mind, the ARW looked to establish a diving section within the unit shortly after it was established. In 1982 Captain Traolach Sweeney took up the mantle. He was already a Defence Forces sports diving instructor, which meant that the unit had one of the country's best and most experienced swimmers as a training instructor.

As with the formation of the unit as a whole, the diving section had a number of glitches on formation. Diving equipment relevant to specialist military diving operations was not available to buy off the shelf and those forming the team had to spend time seeking out suitable equipment, filling out the correct purchase orders and submitting them to the appropriate department for purchase. The tendering process for such equipment was fraught with setbacks, as refusals, corrections and returned forms continuously delayed the process of establishing the section.

Furthermore, what the section got was not always what they ordered. For example, an initial requirement for the section was a number of black drysuits. However, when the consignment arrived, the soldiers were surprised to discover that they were Viking red. The colour was of course unsuitable for covert operations. In order to continue, special black rubber paint was ordered, but, in a further setback, the tins never materialised. In the end, the unit, like many army units, decided to make do with the red suits for the time being.

In time, the section did get the necessary supplies: eight

full sets of diving gear were purchased, along with torches, watches, waterproof gear bags and one petrol compressor. Moreover, two members of the unit, T. Sweeney and Brendan Mallen, travelled to the Avon factory in Wales in March 1983 to examine and choose suitable craft for the unit. Two boats, 5.5 metre Sea-Riders with twin Yamaha 60 outboard engines, were ordered. The boats, the first of their type in Ireland, were fitted with self-righting gear, a device that, when activated, enabled a boat that had turned over to right itself. On completion of their task in Wales, Sweeney and Mallen travelled on to London, where they collected underwater weapon-carrying bags. These were sealed with a custom-made drysuit zip and were specially devised, like all the other items for the section, for the task in hand.

Once the equipment arrived, training began in earnest. The plan was to extend some basic training to the section before sending them on to the Naval Service for a more advanced diving course with a military content. Corporals Tom Cole and Terry O'Leary were assigned as coxswains (the person who steers a ship) to the two Sea-Riders. Those listed for the first training course were T. Sweeney, B. Mallen, Frank Faughnan, Eddie Whitford, Mark Mc, Dennis Dennehy and Noel Hutchinson. Before the Naval Service course commenced, the section was dispatched to Tralee, Co. Kerry, where they began diving training at Fenit pier.

On 20 July 1983 the first ARW combat diver's course was conducted by the Naval Service. The instructors – experienced naval divers – put the candidates through their paces with long runs in drysuits, mud runs and bridge jumping from various heights. Personnel quickly developed a close affinity with the dark and cold waters of Ireland, spending extended periods below the waves.

Modules on the course included physical exercise, fin swimming, endurance life-line diving, jackstay-marked diving (a procedure conducted by divers swimming along a fixed search line termed the jackstay), ship bottom searches and search techniques, compass swimming by day and night, combat swimming, beach landings and clearing drills, and small boat handling. The group was also instructed in the use of explosives under water.

This initial course was the beginning of a long-standing relationship between the ARW and the Naval Service that is still evident today. Both groups work together to test equipment, and research and develop the unit's challenging marine role.

From that course in 1983, and through the decades that have followed, the syllabus has been altered and updated to take in the changing face of warfare and covert seaborne techniques. Current diving equipment includes Dräger LAR VII Rebreathers and STIDD Diver Propulsion Devices. For stealth water insertion, the unit possesses a number of Klepper MK13 kayaks and Nautiraid Mark VI kayaks. For rapid insertion, the ARW uses Zodiac M9 inflatable boats, CRRCs and rigid-hulled inflatable boats.

Combat diving is a very important aspect of the unit's response capacity, and today the ARW has a dive team that is comparable to the finest in the world and whose skills are continually being developed through cross-training with a number of its European counterparts.

18

DROP ZONE

The helicopter has given special forces operatives a useful and viable option for insertions into AOs by parachute. Virtually all soldiers involved in specialist missions are airborne qualified, so as to retain the option of covert tactical insertions by air. Parachuting is also a training tool that builds confidence and develops a unit's *esprit de corps* ('the spirit of the body', i.e. a feeling of pride and loyalty shared by a group).

Since the formation of the ARW, all operatives have been required to undergo a five-jump basic parachute course. This gave the Defence Forces a number of qualified airborne troops, as well as giving those who showed an aptitude for parachuting the chance to progress onto free fall and tactical jumping.

The first Irish Defence Forces parachute course commenced in 1980, providing the Irish Army with airborne capabilities. Later that same year, the first parachute course for the ARW was organised. The chief instructor was John Walsh, an officer who was an experienced parachutist, having been involved in the sport for many years. The Irish Army does not have a dedicated airborne unit, but in 1972 a parachuting club for members of the Defence Forces, called 'An Para-Chumann Mileata' (PCM) and based in the Cadet School at the Curragh Camp, was founded by Platoon Commander Con McNamara. The club invested in a number of ex-US Air Force C-9 parachutes, with the Air Corps using the Curragh Plains for jump training. By 1979 the Air Corps had fitted two Cessna 172s with para modifications that were also sourced from the United States.

ARW parachute training was a joint effort between the unit and the PCM. Con McNamara, John Walsh and Gerry O'Leary conducted courses in Gormanstown. Lectures, supervised packing, organising the manifest and assisting students all came under the watchful eye of these three men and their staff. Along with the seriousness of training specialist operatives, there was an abundance of humour. John Walsh's laugh is remembered by many, as he watched the biggest and toughest Rangers being reduced to quivering wrecks at the first glimpse of the small green Cessna aircraft from which they were expected to jump.

The importance of parachute training amongst the Defence Forces was noted by successive commanding officers and directors of training, resulting in the increase of military parachuting training skills. In 1987 thirty new T-10 military round rigs were purchased, which allowed the parachute school to run a larger course for the permanent Defence Forces (PDF) and the ARW. During the summer months of 1987 instructors began conducting regular progression and display training, using both military and civilian aircraft. This training gave the ARW the ability to insert a five-man team accurately and covertly into an AO. The same skills used by the ARW are similar to those used in a display jump, resulting in many operatives representing the Defence Forces at national and international events.

For many years parachute displays have been a central part in the Defence Forces' public relations portfolio. Unknown to many, some of those participating in these jumps are ARW operatives jumping as part of the PCM's display team: The Black Knights. These displays include air shows, festivals, sports events and community games.

As soldiers completed parachute training, the importance of having such trained troops was noted, resulting in the upgrading of equipment and training. In the late 1990s the PCM secured funding for twenty military-specification square student canopies. These rigs were capable of being used in High Altitude Low Opening (HALO) free-fall training. A unit instructor travelled to the United Kingdom to refit the older systems to the new standard. The HALO technique is an excellent special forces military skill that enables one to jump from over 30,000 feet. Soldiers can fly for up to seventy miles before opening their chute at low altitude and inserting covertly into their AO.

In 2000 three senior instructors travelled to Sweden to test out these rigs for special forces use. The course also qualified the three jump masters to dispatch special forces teams from medium and large military aircraft, including the C-130 Hercules. During the course, the team also compiled the first draft of the 'Manual of Military Parachuting for the Defence Forces'.

The progression rig javelin system is used by jump masters when training students. This smaller and lighter chute allows ease of movement in the confines of an aircraft. Operatives are required to complete sixty jumps with the AFF Rig Zerox training parachute before advancing to using the SOV/MMS-360 FOR MFF system. Manufactured by Thomas Defence Systems, these rigs are of a high and robust standard that suits the rigours of specialist training.

Once fully trained, the primary insertion rig used by operators is the Special Operations Vector Multi Mission System. This rig consists of an MS-360 Silhouette Main Canopy with a maximum deployment altitude of 25,000 feet. The Special Operations Vector Tandem Sigma System, which is also in use today, allows the ARW to insert non-para qualified personnel, such as doctors, support staff and experts in special subject matter, into AOs. This system has a Tandem Phoenix 400 main canopy that also gives a maximum deployment altitude of 25,000 feet.

ARW teams have made daring airborne entries into various diplomatic and military functions over the years, one being a high-powered jump into the American ambassador's residence in the Phoenix Park, Dublin. This rapid deployment and covert insertion into an area deemed impenetrable reveals just one of the unit's methods of gaining entry into an AO.

19

CLOSE QUARTER BATTLE

With the increase in urbanisation throughout Ireland and the world, the military are constantly adapting to fighting in built-up areas. Close Quarter Battle (CQB) is a tactical concept that involves teams or individuals engaging enemy combatants at very short ranges. Because enemy combatants, civilians and fellow operatives can be closely intermingled, CQB demands a rapid assault and precise application of lethal force. Though CQB is not synonymous with urban warfare, the ARW is trained for various urban combat scenarios, which includes hostage rescue.

Operatives need a great proficiency with an array of weapons and the ability to make split-second decisions in order to accomplish the mission. The marksmanship of operatives is honed on a number of indoor and outdoor ranges. To simulate movement of an actual person, the ranges have the facility for a target to be placed on rails so that they move or pop up. ARW personnel can be expected to fire thousands of rounds on these ranges in the process of developing extraordinarily rapid reflexes and an uncanny ability to almost instantly appraise an immediate tactical situation. Having reached a very high standard, they are then moved on to a more realistic setting.

Within its complex at the Curragh Camp, the unit has a number of 'kill houses'. A 'kill' or 'shoot' house is a specially constructed indoor firing range modified to resemble a residential or industrial environment, with walls and floors fortified to safely absorb rounds from close range. Within each 'kill house' a sophisticated camera system records what happens within the confines of the building. Film footage can be replayed later, enabling operatives to watch themselves assaulting the house. These premises can be constructed from a variety of materials, ranging from concrete to plywood, depending on the users of the 'kill house'. Those that need to contain and absorb gunfire, for example, tend to be made from stronger materials such as concrete or ballistic rubber. Exact replicas of buildings may be made that represent entry and access points, windows, corridors and rooms.

The team practices several methods of breaching the house. Specially adapted vehicles enable the unit to storm a building from different levels, for example, while fast roping from a helicopter onto a building can enable a team to enter from the roof. Smoke and pyrotechnic devices are also often used during breach entry to distract.

Once inside, operatives practise breaching wood and

metal doors and walls, as well as moving through rooms while distinguishing armed targets from non-combatants. For this phase of the training, operatives are equipped with weapons that fire a version of a paintball that registers whether the correct target was hit with the pellet of paint. These simulated munitions help provide for a safe environment in which to train.

The purpose of the exercise is to finely hone the individual ARW operator's weapon and firing skills, including shooting on the move, rapid magazine changes and malfunction clearance procedures, as well as rapid target identification and acquisition, and accurate shot placement impacting on the body line.

Operatives initially train in two-man teams to breach an entry, clear a room and secure an area. It is imperative that both operators work in unison, with each soldier communicating through their comms as well as via hand signals. After the entry, be it through a door, window or wall, the team moves in with weapons poised. The weapon is held so that the operator moves his body rather than the weapon to scan arcs and cover all aspects of a room or corridor. While the operatives will have studied a plan of the layout beforehand, working their way through a structure is a daunting and difficult task. Enemy targets need to be engaged without harming a hostage or hostages. The scenario may dictate that the captive requires medical assistance. The team's medic will be on hand to provide this while others provide over-watch and prepare for exfil. Each room needs to be cleared so that the team can egress and exit without endangering the team or those they have rescued.

These types of drills are practised day and night until the operative can execute them with the utmost precision.

As they progress through their training, teams get larger, and in some exercises multiple teams assault a building from different entry points. Complicated scenarios are devised to test the capabilities of the unit.

Unlike conventional military personnel, the ARW operatives wear equipment that has been adapted by the individual. Each mission is different and the operatives wear their personal equipment to suit their needs. For CQB, however, all operatives tend to wear body armour with a Modular Lightweight Load-Carrying Equipment (MOLLE) system of pouches securing spare magazines and comms equipment. A sidearm is also worn via a holster. The layout of an operative's equipment allows them ease of access for each item, as time is often an important factor.

The Irish Defence Forces have built a 360° purpose-built range using ballistic rubber bricks that enables the ARW to use live rounds. Paper silhouettes and mannequins are positioned throughout the building, giving the teams recognisable targets to engage with live fire. On entering the building, operatives have their own rooms or areas to clear and secure, and each operator has his own arc of fire. He must be adept at calculating his arc of fire to encompass the area in which he is operating. For example, if one is in a corridor, the field of fire becomes limited and consequently the arc of fire is reduced. The operator needs to adapt to this in moments.

Moving through the labyrinth of corridors, the operatives are confronted by closed doors. Behind each one is a possible threat. The rooms must be approached and cleared under cover of their teammates. Once inside a room, the arcs must cover 360° for all-round defence, as there is always the threat of being engaged from behind.

This state-of-the-art 360° range can be adapted to suit a number of scenarios, giving the operatives a realistic training facility that enables them to hone their skills, as well as helping them develop new ones.

All of this training, has led to the ARW being field leaders in CQB.

20

BÍ ÚLLAMH[1]

In order to be prepared for any scenario, a unit must be equipped with the proper kit and vehicles for both covert and overt operations. For operating covertly, the ARW is equipped with Nissan Patrols, Ford Rangers, Nissan Navaras and Range Rovers that can be adapted to the required mission specifications. For off-road work there are also a range of multi-terrain vehicles, such as the Yamaha 660, KTM motorcycles and the Suzuki DR350 and DR-Z400 motorcycles. Meanwhile, for overt operations, the unit drives a number of Ford F-350 SRVs equipped with Weapons Mount Installation Kits (WMIK). The unit also uses a number of French ACMAT VLRA as tactical support vehicles for resupplying the SRVs.

The ARW has access to a veritable arsenal of weapons that, once again, cover all mission requirements. These include personal and support weapons, as well as vehicle-mounted systems. Operatives adapt their personal

---

1 'Be prepared.'

equipment to suit their needs, balancing self-protection with efficiency by using vests that hold ballistic plates, ammunition and comms.

Whether operating at home or abroad, the unit is capable of adapting to any and all mission requirements.

Recent domestic missions have included aiding the civil power by helping provide security for Queen Elizabeth II's visit to Ireland in 2011, where a viable threat from dissident republicans resulted in three Agusta-Westland AW139 helicopters with sniper teams on board flying overhead and counter-assault teams shadowing the motorcade. Operatives were also deployed in ground teams that included twenty CP officers.

Two years later the ARW formed part of the security apparatus for Ireland's six-month presidency of the Council of the European Union. It provided sniper and spotter teams at locations where talks were being held. Also in 2013, in June, the unit assisted in securing border areas on land and sea during the G8 summit in Fermanagh.

In recent years, the ARW has conducted a number of exercises in Ireland as an aid to the civil power. However, with Taoiseach Varadkar's creation of a new Government Security Committee in 2017, also known as 'Cabinet Committee F', it was decided to give a more direct and high-profile role to the ARW in responding to the threat of international terrorism spreading to Ireland. Exercises were devised to be centred on how the Defence Forces would respond to a 'major on-island terrorist incident'. Working with the gardaí, ambulance and fire service, and other response agencies, the ARW has developed agreed protocols, command and control, crisis management and timed responses. By working together, both the Defence Forces and An Garda Síochána have built on their capabilities and developed their procedures.

Exercises consist of the ARW, the Naval Service and the Air Corps, along with the gardaí, working together. In one example, the ARW deployed assault teams by sea and air onto the Stena Superfast Ferry before securing the vessel as it approached Dublin Port. Naval ships and an Air Corps CASA aircraft located and monitored the vessel in Irish waters, while ARW assault teams boarded the ferry from AW139 helicopters and RIBs. Gardaí, along with military command, oversaw the exercise, with the guards being on standby to assist the military in arranging roadblocks and cordon security.

Other exercises include deployments with regular army units at Dublin Airport and Dublin Port. Various operational and tactical procedures are undertaken during the exercises, with an emphasis on the ARW working in co-operation with An Garda Síochána's Emergency Response Unit and Armed Response Unit, who are currently the front-line units for dealing with a domestic terrorist attack.

Working together on these exercises ensures that any potential threats can be contained and eliminated. The capabilities of the gardaí and the military, from command and control to ground forces, are considerable, and while such exercises usually take place out of the public eye, they do provide a force multiplier.

Internationally, the ARW is well regarded not only for its marksmanship capabilities but also for its UN deployments, which have seen the unit operate in numerous inhospitable environments alongside its counterparts.

The ARW is set to assume an increasing role in the global conflicts of the twenty-first century, ensuring that it will continue to be on the front line, adapting, as always, to changing circumstances. As part of the Irish government's commitment to the Common Security and Defence Policy (CSDP), the Irish Defence Forces have been involved in EU battle-groups for a number of years. It is planned that, in 2020, as part of a German-led battle-group, the Irish Defence Forces will deploy a unit comprising a C2 group (Command & Control), the ARW, Explosive Ordnance Disposal (EOD), engineers, and a force protection element, along with a logistical and administration group. This deployment will enhance the ARW's inter-operability, challenge its leadership and lead to the development of additional skill sets. It will also help develop relationships with key international partners and give the ARW an opportunity to operate in an international environment where it will be at the cutting edge of special forces operations.

CONCLUSION

Because the ARW is not in the public eye, many do not even know of the existence of this unit or its capabilities. Though The Wing has remained a covert group within the Irish Defence Forces, those who are serving or who have passed through the ranks of the unit have, like the Fianna of old, protected the state and its people from foreign and domestic threats. They have also assisted those in peril overseas, adding to the unit's honour. This has come at a high price, with four operatives losing their lives while on active service.[1]

Although the capabilities and the equipment of the ARW have evolved since 1980, one aspect of the unit has remained constant: the maintenance of exceptionally high standards. Its success as a unit is not down to the high-tech equipment and weaponry at its disposal, though it does have recourse to such hardware. Rather it is because of the wide-ranging training each ARW operative receives, covering every aspect of warfare, coupled with

---

1   The names of those killed have been omitted from the text at the request of the Irish Defence Forces. They are remembered on a memorial located within the ARW compound at the Curragh Camp.

each operative's physical and mental determination to get the job done.

However, in the end, the cornerstone of the ARW is the individual soldier and their determination to be the best of the best.

APPENDIX

'SO, YOU WANT TO PASS SELECTION ...'

THE DECISION

It is crucial that your reasons for undergoing selection are clear-cut because at some stage you *are* going to ask yourself: 'What the hell am I doing here?' If you have a good answer, you will be able to dig deep and continue, no matter how hard and painful things become.

Assuming the above is true, you now face the biggest challenge of your career, if not your life, as the course is designed to test your physical and mental strength to the limit. Everything else must take a back seat or you *will* fail.

PHYSICAL PREPARATION

The test phase of selection, which takes place during the first, instructional, week, examines all aspects of your physical potential through a 10-kilometre road run in running gear, cross-country speed marches of various distances over different types of terrain with reduced Combat Equipment Marching Order (CEMO) (35 pounds +) and rifle, cross-country marches of varying distances over mountainous terrain with CEMO (45 pounds +) and rifle, and gym tests to assess speed, agility and upper-body strength.

The make-or-break tactics phase lasts two weeks, during which you will be continuously carrying heavy loads, including everything you will need to live on for two weeks on the ground, plus group equipment such as radios, spare batteries, night vision equipment (NVE), ammunition, etc.

The arduous physical challenges presented by terrain, weather, the 'enemy' and heavy loads, will be compounded by minimal sleep and poor food.

PRE-TRAINING

Seek the advice of people you know who have undergone selection in the last couple of years.

Aim to finish your training about a week before the course so as to allow a rest period.

There are no rules for achieving your highest level of fitness, as everybody is different. However, the following may help. Identify your strengths and weaknesses and, with the help of a PTI, design a programme that reflects your needs.

Record your fastest time over two miles and 10 kilometres and your maximum push-ups and sit-ups in a minute. Test yourself regularly to see if you are improving. Keep a training log.

Vary your training to keep it interesting and train with like-minded individuals where possible. Much of your training may have to be done outside working hours, if your normal working day doesn't allow for PT.

Gradually introduce combat PT into your training, initially in runners before progressing to boots. Start by carrying around 10 pounds and increase this in 5-pound increments.

Ideally, train six days a week (four days minimum) and put aside one for rest (often your most important day's training).

Listen to your body. For example, if your legs begin to ache from too much running, do another form of training, or rest completely. Avoid contact sports to lessen the risk of injury.

EQUIPMENT

Equipment can be an important factor, but you don't have to spend a fortune. Most of the general issue kit will suffice, provided you keep it in good condition and it fits you properly. Constantly use and familiarise yourself with your kit, from your thermal tops and socks, through to the way you wear your CEMO.

Five pairs of good mountain socks, seamless and

well padded around the soles, will prove to be a wise investment. If your budget can stretch to a cold-weather jacket, a Buffalo or Snug Pack type is ideal.

Bring two skip caps, a pair of good leather gloves, thermal inner gloves, and a head-over or thermal scarf.

Bring two pairs of well broken-in boots: good-quality sports insoles will help prevent injury. During the tactics phase, Gore-Tex boots and Gore-Tex/Seal Skin-type socks are essential.

Another vital part of your equipment is webbing, i.e. a strong fabric woven and used for military strapping and apparel. Incorrectly fitted webbing can cause injury, as well as making your life miserable. Your battle vest needs to fit like a glove, as you will be wearing it almost continuously throughout the course. Also make sure you get your pack fitted for your body size.

When happy with your MOLLE system configurations, pack them as you would for the course (this will be covered in depth during the prelims) and use them during training to get used to wearing them and carrying the weight.

Given all the above, keep the following at the forefront of your mind: if you want to pass, you will take the first step; if you want to pass, you will prepare; if you want to pass, you *will*!

BIBLIOGRAPHY

BOOKS/PAMPHLETS

Ranger Syllabus of Training (Irish Defence Forces Printing Press, Dublin, 1969)

1st Defence Forces Ranger Course: 40th Anniversary Celebration (Irish Defence Forces Printing Press, Dublin, 2009)

Army Ranger Wing – 21st Anniversary Paper (Irish Defence Forces Printing Press, Dublin, 2001)

MAGAZINES

An Cosantóir

The New Yorker

RECOMMENDED READING

Reading these books, as well as others, enables preparation for whatever is to come. The study of military history and leadership offers an inexpensive chance to learn from the experience of others. It will enable you to form a template for solving challenges that you will encounter in your profession. By reading, reflecting and learning, you will increase your understanding of our history, the global situation and the enduring lessons of war.

Beckworth, C. A., *Delta Force: A Memoir by the Founder of the U.S. Military's Most Secretive Special Operations Unit* (William Morrow Paperbacks, New York, 2013)

Blaber, P., *The Mission, The Men, and Me: Lessons from a former Delta Force Commander* (Caliber, Illinois, 2010)

Fick, N., *One Bullet Away: The Making of a Marine Officer* (Mariner Books, New York, 2006)

Fiennes, R., *Mad, Bad and Dangerous to Know* (Hodder & Stoughton, London, 2008)

Fowler, W., *Operation Barras: The SAS Rescue Mission, Sierra Leone 2000* (Cassell, London, 2007)

Haney E. L., *Inside Delta Force: The Story of America's Elite Counterterrorist Unit* (Delacorte Press, New York, 2007)

Lewis, R., *Company Commander* (Virgin Books, London, 2013)

McChrystal, S., *Team of Teams: New Rules of Engagement for a Complex World* (Portfolio, New York, 2015)

McRaven, W. H., *Spec Ops: Case Studies in Special Operations Warfare Theory and Practice* (Presidio Press, New York, 1996)

Murray, S., *Legionnaire: An Englishman in the French Foreign Legion* (Pan Books, London, 2003)

Naylor, S., *Not a Good Day to Die: The Untold Story of Operation Anaconda* (Caliber, Illinois, 2006)

Sinek, S., *Leaders Eat Last: Why Some Teams Pull Together and Others Don't* (Portfolio Penguin, New York, 2014)

Smith, M., *An Unsung Hero: Tom Crean – Antarctic Survivor* (Collins Press, Cork, 2010)

Urban, M., *Task Force Black* (St Martin's Press, London, 2012)

ACKNOWLEDGEMENTS

This book is a collaboration. In researching and writing *Shadow Warriors*, Sergeant Wayne Fitzgerald and I became immersed in the clandestine world of the Irish Special Forces. As a result, many people have contributed to its contents. Because of the nature of this topic and the many permissions needed to research, write and bring the finished article to the reader, a lengthy period of time elapsed. During this period, there have been many changes in command, but without the support of those past and present, we would never have completed this work. The Irish Defence Forces and the Department of Defence granted us permission for the project and permitted us access to the unit and its operatives. For that we are very grateful.

We acknowledge the assistance of the current chief of staff, Vice-Admiral Mark Mellett DSM; Major General Kieran Brennan, who was the deputy chief of staff operations (now retired) and his successor Major General Anthony McKenna; OiC Public Relations Branch Lieutenant Colonel Oliver Dwyer (now O/C 60th Infantry Group UNDOF) and his successor, Lieutenant Colonel Johnny

Whittaker; O/C Information Office Commandant Colin Lawlor (now Military College) and his successor Commandant David McKnight; and Sergeant Rena Kennedy, Defence Forces Press Office. We would especially like to acknowledge the assistance of the current and past O/C of the ARW and his senior NCOs.

We discovered that within the world of special forces – not only in Ireland, but throughout the world – there is a brotherhood and a code of silence. We have at all times respected this code and appreciate those who allowed us access and provided us with the inside story of the ARW. All the soldiers who contributed to this book were patient and generous with their time. They have at all times been of great assistance, and without their collaboration this book would never have been written. For security reasons many of those who have aided us in this venture, both serving and ex members of the unit and those associated with the ARW, remain nameless.

For her professional advice and for reading the initial drafts we would like to thank Dr Mary Montaut.

We are most grateful to the staff of the Military Archives in Dublin for their assistance throughout the writing of this book and for those soldiers who gave us their experiences on SAG training.

We would especially like to thank retired Battalion Quartermaster Sergeant Stephen Rynn for information provided on his service overseas with the Irish Defence Forces.

Many thanks to all the staff in *An Cosantóir* for their continuous support, especially their archivist Mr Séan Shinners.

We would like to thank all at Mercier Press, in particular Patrick O'Donoghue, Noel O'Regan, Wendy Logue, Sarah O'Flaherty, Deirdre Roberts and Mary Feehan.

On a personal note, moral support came from both our families and friends, including my wife Marian and daughter Bláthnaid. Wayne's wife Sharon and family also supported us on this venture. For encouragement in the line of fire, thanks go to Liz Gillis, Micheál O'Doibhlín, Las Fallon, Ronnie Daly, John Galligan and Lar Joye. Special thanks also to my parents, Thomas and Rita O'Brien, for their continuous support.

The ARW operatives Wayne and I encountered are audacious and brave, and work best when totally unfettered. We thank each and every one of them, including those who remain unnamed, and their families, for their forbearance and their service to our country.

Little is known or has been written about Ireland's specialist military capabilities and it is hoped that *Shadow Warriors* will go some way towards addressing this shortfall.

Paul O'Brien
Sergeant Wayne Fitzgerald